FOLK SONGS

OF THE

SOUTHERN

APPALACHIANS

Second Edition

FOLK SONGS OF THE
SOUTHERN
APPALACHIANS

AS SUNG BY

Jean
Ritchie

Second Edition

Forewords by
Alan Lomax
and Ron Pen

THE UNIVERSITY PRESS OF KENTUCKY

Publication of this volume was made possible in part
by a grant from the National Endowment for the Humanities.

Scholarly publisher for the Commonwealth,
serving Bellarmine College, Berea College, Centre
College of Kentucky, Eastern Kentucky University,
The Filson Club Historical Society, Georgetown College,
Kentucky Historical Society, Kentucky State University,
Morehead State University, Murray State University,
Northern Kentucky University, Transylvania University,
University of Kentucky, University of Louisville,
and Western Kentucky University.

Editorial and Sales Offices: The University Press of Kentucky
663 South Limestone Street, Lexington, Kentucky 40508-4008

01 00 99 98 97   5 4 3 2 1

ISBN 0-8131-2021-7
ISBN 0-8131-0927-2 (paper)

Contents

Foreword to the Second Edition
by Ron Pen

Opening the cover of Jean Ritchie's *Folk Songs of the Southern Appalachians* is like being welcomed into a cosy living room filled with family gathered by the warm hearth. Turning the pages, you are drawn into the vibrant life of Balis and Abigail Ritchie's family, told through songs, stories, and photographs that sing of a life lived in the mountains of eastern Kentucky at a time when railroads, coal mines, and hillbilly radio were making their first incursions. One page bubbles with the squeals of children playing a game while singing "The Old Soap Gourd." Turn the page and you encounter an emotional baptism in the river accompanied by the haunting strains of "Guide Me, Oh Thou Great Jehovah." Yet another page finds Jean and her sisters busily stringing popcorn while humming "Old King Cole." Each page illuminates a poignant aspect of daily life and work while revealing the inextricable relationship between life and music in this remarkable family.

It is slightly more than thirty years now since Jean Ritchie's *Folk Songs of the Southern Appalachian Mountains* was first issued by Oak Publications. Fondly known by the folk community as "the blue book," because of its distinctive cover, Ritchie's collection of Child ballads, lyric folksongs, play party and frolic songs, native American ballads, Old Regular Baptist lined hymns, "hant" songs, and carols embodies the heart of the unique "Singing Ritchie Family" repertoire. Built upon a foundation of balladry inherited from old-world Scotland, the family embraced new songs from a wide variety of sources including settlement schools, records, neighbors, church, and radio. The Ritchies were old-fashioned enough to cherish and retain their legacy of inherited songs but modern enough to appreciate and absorb the new influences of popular music.

The family repertoire was eclectic, but it was certainly not haphazard. This is a collection consciously assembled by collectors, fashioned by an uncommon family. Jean, her father Balis, and her "Uncle" Jason were not simply passive bearers of tradition. They were "song hunters" who actively sought out, collected, and arranged versions of music. Seeking the best versions of ballads, completing incomplete fragments, assembling complementary verses from different sources, and adding or embellishing tunes were essential to preserving a complete and comprehensible version that would eventually pass into the family's collection of shared song. Jean's description of her father's activity in *Singing Family of the Cumberlands* best describes this process: "I guess it was Dad, though, who was the biggest song hunter of us all, besides Uncle Jason. Especially around the time he got his printing press and took a notion to put out his little songbook, *Lover's Melodies* (1910-11). He used to tell me, 'I'd hear a part of a song, and if I liked it, I'd learn all that fellow knew of it, and then I'd travel amongst the people of the country here and learn one part from one and another from another until I had the whole song.'"

Jean's Uncle Jason, a lawyer by trade, was also a "song hunter" who was especially known for his repertoire of "big" ballads—the narrative songs collected and canonized by Francis Child. Jean absorbed both her father and Uncle Jason's songs and then expanded her own collection through attentive listening and study culminating in the year spent in Britain collecting folklore under the auspices of a Fulbright Grant in 1952. The music found in *Folk Songs of the Southern Appalachians* represents the traditional family repertoire that "sang up the moon" on the front porch, but this collection also represents some of the most highly polished and artfully sculpted versions of the Appalachian art.

This new edition from the University Press of Kentucky is faithful to the original Oak Publication in every respect. All seventy-seven songs are represented in the line scores transcribed by Melinda Zacuto and Jerry Silverman. While the notation is reasonably accurate, even the most detailed transcription would fail to capture the flexibility and florid ornamentation of lined hymns such as "The Day Is Past and Gone." Simple chordal indications are provided to facilitate guitar or autoharp accompaniment, except in the case of ballads and Old Regular Baptist hymns where chords would be inappropriate or where they might disrupt the modal harmony.

The wonderful headnotes introducing each song have all been retained. Jean's comments draw you into the life of the song and provide a wealth of informal yet informed background on the social and historical context for the music. Likewise, all of the original photographs accompanying the pictures have been reproduced from negatives hunted up in, as Jean says "various and often surprising corners of our rambling house." The photos, taken by Jean's husband George Pickow, present a vibrant and intimate portrait of the family. His images are visually striking and effectively complement the songs with which they are paired.

While nothing has been eliminated from the original, several important additions have been made to this edition. Four new songs have been inserted, including three that have not previously been published: *Loving Hannah, Lovin' Henry,* and *Her Mantle So Green.* An additional song, *The Reckless and Rambling Boy,* was previously published in a shorter version in *Celebration of Life* (1971). *Loving Hannah,* recorded early in Jean's career (1953) and again in 1995 on *Mountain Born,* is a haunting lyric folk song enjoying contemporary popularity through the performance of Irish singer Mary Black. *Lovin' Henry* is the Ritchie version of the Child ballad depicting the treacherous woman who lured Henry to infidelity and death. *Her Mantle So Green* exemplifies Jean's process of folk adaptation and arrangement. Inheriting only a fragment of the Irish song from her Uncle Jason, she subsequently reconstructed the song through additional collected verses and some original composition. *The Reckless and Rambling Boy* likewise is an arrangement compounded of versions learned from her father, Uncle Jason, and Perry County banjo player Justus Begley. Her version is particularly interesting because it provides some of the narrative fabric and motivation missing from the closely related lyric folksong *Black Is the Color.*

Music notation and the printed word can only present a reasonable facsimile of any actual song. Jean's singing is simply the best guide to how the song should be sung. For that reason, a new audiography and videography of current sources has been compiled to facilitate access to the recorded versions of the music. Many of the songs are currently available, but other "out-of-print" recordings can be located in public and university libraries. The discography appended to Karen Carter-Schwendler's Ph.D. dissertation, "Traditional Background, Contemporary Context: The Music and Activities of Jean Ritchie to 1977" (University of Kentucky, 1995), provides an efficient means for identifying recordings that are no longer available.

Jean Ritchie is celebrating fifty years of public performance. It is fifty years since she made her first recording, *The Two Sisters*, for the Library of Congress Archive of Folksong and fifty years since she made her debut concert appearance at an alumni tea for New York University. In the intervening years, Jean has confirmed her status as a consummate musician and author through the publication of ten books and the release of more than forty recordings. Her performances at concerts and festivals throughout the world have sparked the dulcimer revival, and her original songs, such as *Black Waters, The L&N Don't Stop Here Anymore,* and *Now Is the Cool of the Day*, are among the most affective and popular additions to the folk repertory. Thus it is most appropriate that the University Press of Kentucky celebrate this remarkable talent by republishing *Folk Songs of the Southern Appalachians*. This collection contains the very essence of home, hearth, and porch family life—the heart of Jean Ritchie's music and career.

1996

Foreword
by Alan Lomax

Ballad singing, like talent for music in general, often runs in families. There were the Bachs of Germany, good at Chorales and counterpoint. There were the MacCrimmons of Skye, who were good at pibroch and taught all Scotland the "big music" of the bagpipes. There are the Smiths of the Shenandoah Valley, who have spread the ballads to the west from Virginia to Kansas. And in Kentucky, two of the great ballad-singing families were the Combses of Knott County and the Ritchies of Perry County. The family ballads of the Combses formed the basis of the first scholarly book on the British ballad in America, done by Professor Josiah Combs as a doctor's thesis for the Sorbonne and published in Paris. In Jean Ritchie's book, *Singing Family of the Cumberlands*, the prolific ballad-singing Ritchie tribe achieved a rich and colorful family portrait. Jean Ritchie's own songbook serves as a musical companion for the Ritchie family book, and contains some prime Ritchie songs; and that is to say, you won't find anywhere a better batch of Appalachian mountain songs.

One of the Ritchies fought the Redcoats in 1776. Then he moved his family back up into the rugged hills and notches of Eastern Kentucky, where the water was clear and there were still elk in the woods. His folks helped to organize county governments and start schools. When the Civil War came along, most of the Ritchies fought on the Union side. They were quiet, thoughtful folks, who went in for ballads and big families and educating their children. Jean's grandmother was a prime mover in the neighborhood Old Regular Baptist Church, and all the traditional hymn tunes came from her. Jean's Uncle Jason was a lawyer and historian who remembers the big ballads like "Lord Barnard." Jean's father taught school, printed a newspaper, fitted specs, farmed, and sent ten of his fourteen children to college.

Jean is the youngest of the fourteen. By the time she came along, her older sisters had already gone over the ridges to Pine Mountain Settlement School, where among other things the youngsters were taught to "appreciate their own." There had always been a great deal of singing in the Ritchie house—in the kitchen, on the turnrow in the corn field, or while the babies were being patted to sleep on the big bed. But when the girls came home from Pine Mountain for their Christmas holidays, the family sing-songs turned into feasts for the ballad hunter. The sweet old carols treasured up from England, the new frolic tunes of the American frontier—all were trotted out and admired and polished by this family as they sat and sang on their front porch up on Elk Branch in Viper, Kentucky. That's where Jean Ritchie drank in her folk music right from the clear eye of the spring. Certainly Jean's family do not think of her as a remarkable singer. Yet Jean's quiet, serene, objective voice, the truth of her pitch, the perfection and restraint of her decorations (the shakes and quavers that fall upon the melody to suit it to the poetry) all denote a superb mountain singer. Jean's long residence in the city and as queen on all folksinging platforms across the country has not stained the original purity of her style. On the contrary, she has matured as a singer in the past two decades of professional work, adding polish, but more important, command of the full resources of traditional techniques for variation and embellishment of the songs to her original fine style. She has, besides, become a scholar and collector of folklore, folk instruments, and folk music. If you wish to sing Appalachian songs well, get hold of her records and follow her lead, note by note, because her style shows the way the songs should be sung.

The songs themselves, ranging from the true folk version of "Black is the Color," through the best of "Barbara Allen" versions, give the full range of the true backwoods folk song. Having just completed some months of collecting in the British Isles, I can say with assurance that in no one place there will you find such a variety of fine songs as can be found in the repertoire of Jean Ritchie's Kentucky family; for on that front porch in the Kentucky mountains, you will find songs from England, Scotland, and Ireland, as well as new products which represent an apparent fusion of the three.

Instead of providing notes citing other published versions of the songs, Jean Ritchie has put the songs in their proper family setting. The songs have been faithfully transcribed from Jean's singing and, if you must use an instrument, guitar chords have been indicated for most of them. But remember, these songs have always lived without accompaniment or harmony—pure and serene, classic expressions of human feeling.

1965

The Swapping Song

We have always known this "little foolish thing"--Dad's description of "The Swapping Song." Very often it is used for baby-bouncing, because of its jiggy rhythm. According to those that know, however, the song is made up of two old nursery rhymes from the England of one hundred and seventy-five years ago. The verses in the beginning are descended from a little ditty called "The Foolish Boy," all about the little boy going to London to get a wife. The swapping verses which follow this adventure are descended from the original "Swapping Song."

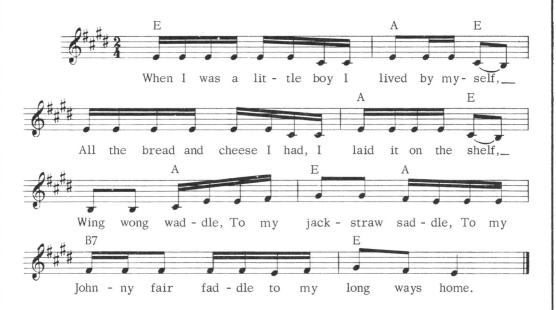

When I was a lit-tle boy I lived by my-self,__
All the bread and cheese I had, I laid it on the shelf,__
Wing wong wad-dle, To my jack-straw sad-dle, To my
John-ny fair fad-dle to my long ways home.

The rats and the mice, they led me such
a life,
I had to go to London to get myself a
wife.

The roads were so long and the lanes
were so narrow,
I had to bring her home in an old wheelbarrow.

The wheelbarrow broke and my wife got
a fall;
Down came wheelbarrow, wife and all.

Swapped my wheelbarrow and got me a
horse;
Then I rode from cross to cross.

Swapped my horse and got me a mare;
Then I rode from fair to fair.

Swapped my mare and got me a mule;
Then I rode like a dog-gone fool.

Swapped my mule and got me a goat;
When I got on him, he wouldn't tote.

Swapped my goat and got me a sheep;
Then I rode myself to sleep.

Swapped my sheep and got me a cow;
And in that trade I just learned how.

Swapped my cow and got me a calf;
In that trade I just lost half.

Swapped my calf and got me a hen;
O, what a pretty thing I had then!

Swapped my hen and got me a rat;
Put it on the haystack away from the cat.

Swapped my rat and got me a mouse;
Its tail caught afire and burned up my
house.

Swapped my mouse and got me a mole;
The dog-gone thing went straight to its
hole.

False Sir John

Another fine "old one" from my singing days with Uncle Jason Ritchie. The "May Colvin" in this song is descended from "Lady Isabel," and her "False Sir John" is known in the older Child ballad as "the Elfknight." Being a woman, I always have liked this one...our hills are full of the beautiful sad laments of maidens loved and deserted. This is one of the few songs in which we get even!

False Sir John a - woo-ing came, To a la-dy young and fair, May Cal-vin was this la-dy's name, And her fa-ther's on-ly heir, Her fa-ther's on-ly heir.

He woo'd her while she spun the
  thread,
And while they made the hay,
Until he gained her low consent
To mount and ride away,
  To mount and ride away.

It's bring-a me some of your father's
  gold
And some of your mother's fee
I'll take thee to some far-off land
And there I'll marry thee,
  And there I'll marry thee.

She's gone into her father's coffer,
Where all of his monies lay,
She's took the yeller and left the white
And lightly skipped away,
  And lightly skipped away.

She's gone into her father's stables
Where all of his steeds did stand,
She's took the best and left the worst
In all of her father's land,
  In all of her father's land.

She's mounted on a milk-white steed
And he on a dapple-grey
And they rode till they come to a
  lonesome spot,
A cliff by the side of the sea.
  A cliff by the side of the sea.

Light down, light down, said false
  Sir John,
Your bridal bed you see,
It's seven women have I drownded here
And the eighth one you shall be,
  And the eighth one you shall be.

Have off, have off your holland smock,
With borders all around,
For it's too costly to lay down
  here
And rot on the cold, cold ground.
  And rot on the cold, cold ground.

Cast off, cast off your silks so fine,
And lay them on a stone,
For they're too fine and cost-i-lie
To rot in the salt sea foam,
  To rot in the salt sea foam.

Take off, take off your silken stays,
Likewise your handsome shoes,
For they're too fine and cost-i-lie
To rot in the sea with you,
  To rot in the sea with you.

Turn around, turn around, thou false
  Sir John,
And look at the leaves on the tree,
For it don't become a gentleman
A naked woman to see,
  A naked woman to see.

Oh false Sir John has turned around
To gaze at the leaves on the tree,
She's made a dash with her tender
  little arms
And pushed him into the sea,
  And pushed him into the sea.

Oh help, oh help, May Colvin,
Oh help or I shall drown,
I'll take thee back to thy father's
  house
And lightly set thee down,
  And lightly set thee down.

No help, no help, said May Colvin,
No help will you get from me,
For the bed's no colder to you sir
Then you thought to give to me,
  Then you thought to give to me.

She mounted on the milk-white steed,
And led the dapple-grey,
And rode till she come to her father's
  house
At the breakin' of the day,
  At the breakin' of the day.

Then up and spoke that little parrot,
Said, May Colvin, where have you been,
And what have you done with false
  Sir John
That went with you ridin',
  That went with you ridin'?

Oh hold your tongue my pretty parrot,
And tell no tales on me,
And I'll buy you a cage of beaten gold
With spokes of i-vor-y,
  With spokes of i-vor-y.

Killy Kranky

Uncle Jason calls this one a play ditty, because according to his description of it, it was both a game and a song and not much of either one. The players sang the song while they "wound the grapevine," using different variations, all of which Uncle Jason avowed was just a good excuse to get their arms around one another. He thought that the words, "Killy Kranky" were just nonsense syllables, and so did I until my husband and I found the town of Killy Kranky (by accident, when we lost the main road) in Scotland!

©1965 by Geordie Music Publishing, Inc.

Kil - ly Kran - ky is my song. Sing and dance it all day long,

From my el - bow to my wrist, Now we do the dou - ble twist.

Broke my arm, broke my arm, a-swing-in' pur - ty Nan - cy,

Broke my leg, I broke my leg, a-danc-in' Kil - ly Kran - ky.

Killy Kranky is my song,
Sing and dance it all day long;
From my wrist down to my knee,
Now we'll wind the grapevine tree.

  Broke my arm, broke my arm,
  A-swingin' pretty Nancy;
  Broke my leg, I broke my leg
  A-dancin' Killy Kranky!

Killy Kranky is my song,
Sing and dance it all day long;
From my knee down to my toe --
How much furder can you go?

  Broke my arm, broke my arm
  A-swingin' pretty Nancy;
  Broke my leg, I broke my leg
  A-dancin' Killy Kranky!

4

Nottamun Town

This song was not, as I remember, ever sung lightly about the house, not even by us girls over the dishpan, but was saved for summer evenings on our long front porch after supper. We knew from the words that it was supposed to be a funny song, but somehow the tune of it was so sadly beautiful, so sort of eerie, that we never felt like laughing whenever we sang it. Since I have travelled through England and have been reading about the roots of our songs, I've learned that "Nottamun Town" is probably an old magic song, a remnant of one of the early mummers' plays, during the playing of which the actors--local village lads all--would turn their clothing inside out and blacken or mask their faces so as not to be recognized by their neighbors. The play itself was a series of magic symbols woven together, and the song words painted topsy-turvy, upside-down-and-backward images. Because, as one old-timer told me, "if 'twas understood, then the good luck and the magic be lost."

Slowly

In fair Not-ta-mun Town, not a soul would look up, Not a soul would look up, not a soul would look down, Not a soul would look up, not a soul would look down, To show me the way to fair Not-ta-mun Town.

I rode a gray horse, a mule-roany mare,
Gray mane and gray tail, green stripe down her back;
Gray mane and gray tail, green stripe down her back,
There wa'nt a hair on her be what was coal black.

She stood so still, she threw me to the dirt,
She tore my hide, and bruised my shirt.
From saddle to stirrup I mounted again
And on my ten toes I rode over the plain.

Met the King and the Queen and a company more,
A-riding behind and a-marching before.
Come a stark-nekkid drummer a-beating a drum,
With his hands in his bosom come marching along.

They laughed and they smiled, not a soul did look gay,
They talked all the while, not a word did they say;
I bought me a quart to drive gladness away,
And to stifle the dust, for it rained the whole day.

Set down on a hard, hot, cold-frozen stone,
Ten thousand stood around me, and yet I'uz alone.
Took my hat in my hands for to keep my head warm.
Ten thousand got drownded that never was born.

Edward

Four of my sisters attended the Hindman Settlement School in Knott County, Kentucky, the school which our Great-Grandfather Solomon Everidge helped to plan and build. One of the many good things about this school and its later companion, the Pine Mountain Settlement School, was their music program. The teachers began by learning the local traditional songs from their mountain pupils, and their song books were compiled from the combined repertoires of all the families round about--a rich and beautiful collection. To this, they added ballads and songs taken from the Child collection and others, different versions of the people's own songs. This of course gave young Kentucky mountaineers a tremendous sense of pride in their inherited music, and an incentive to sing, enjoy and preserve it that many of them would not have otherwise had. For this, we shall always be thankful. The Edward ballad, or, as we called it, "How Came That Blood on Your Shirt Sleeve?" was one of the old-country songs that Una and May learned at Hindman.

Trad. English

Freely, a capella

How came that blood_on your shirt sleeve, Oh dear love, tell me, Well it is the blood_of the old_ gray mare, That ploughed the fields for_ me, me, me, That ploughed the fields for me.

(Part II)

It does look too pale_ for the old grey mare that___ ploughed the fields for_ thee, thee, thee, That ploughed the fields for thee.

How came that blood on your shirt
  sleeve,
Oh dear love, tell me.
Oh it is the blood of the old grey
  hound
That chased the fox for me, -me, -me,
  That chased the fox for me.

(Part II)

It does look too pale for the old grey
  hound
That chased the fox for thee, -thee,
  -thee,
  That chased the fox for thee.

How came that blood on your shirt
   sleeve,
Oh dear love, tell me.
Oh it is the blood of my brother-in-law
That went away with me, -me, -me,
   That went away with me.

(Part II)

And it's what will you do now, my love,
Oh dear love, tell me.
I'll set my foot on yonders ship
And I'll sail across the sea, -sea,
   -sea,
    Sail across the sea.

(Part II)

And it's when will you be back, my
   love,
Oh dear love, tell me.
When the moon sinks yonder in the
   sycamore tree
And that will never be, -be, -be,
   And that will never be.

(Part II)

London Bridge

One of the Halls' girls, our cousin on our mother's side, married and raised a large family on Mace's Creek, one of the major branches that feeds the North Fork of the Kentucky River. This song will serve to illustrate the ever-surprising fact that a song can exist in several different forms within the radius of a few miles, even within the same family. Of course, the commonly known "London Bridge is falling down, my fair lady," learnt in all schools, was sung and played by us all; Uncle Jason's playparty variant goes, "London's bridge is washed away, Dance round, you ladies all!" and our Mace's Creek cousins, the Pratt children, sing, "London Bridge is falling down, my true lover!" All three tunes are quite distinct. Here is my family's adaptation of the Mace's Creek version.

© 1965 by Geordie Music Publishing, Inc.

Lon - don Bridge is fall - ing down, fall - ing down, fall - ing down,

Lon - don Bridge is fall - ing down, My true lov - er.

London Bridge is half fell down,
  Half fell down, half fell down,
London Bridge is half fell down,
  My true lover.

London Bridge is all fell down, (etc.)

London Bridge is half built up.

London Bridge is all built up.

Underneath the prisoner goes.

What's the prisoner done to you?

Stole my golden watch and chain.

What can set him free again?

One hundred pounds and a bag of grain.

Hundred pounds I have not got.

Then off to prison he must go.

Fare you well to London-O.

Sister Phoebe

Mom Ritchie gave us this gentle little kissing game. She says that when she was growing up, dancing was a sin but kissing games were considered "civil and harmless--we even played them in front of the preachers and the old folks and none thought anything against it. Some joined in, too."

Oh, sis - ter Phoe - be, how mer - ry was she, The night she sat un - der the jun - i - per tree. The jun - i - per tree, hi - o, hi - o, The jun - i - per tree, hi - o.

2. Put this hat on your head to keep your
    head warm,
And take a sweet kiss, it will do you no
    harm,
But a great deal of good I'm sure, I'm
    sure,
A great deal of good, I'm sure.

O brother Robert, how merry was he
The night he sat under the juniper tree,
The juniper tree, heigh-o, heigh-o!
The juniper tree, heigh-o!

Put this hat on your head to keep your
    head warm,
And take a sweet kiss, it will do you no
    harm,
But a great deal of good, I'm sure, I'm
sure,
A great deal of good, I'm sure.

Dear Companion

This is one of the beautiful sad songs that sound so pretty on the mountain dulcimer. There are an uncommon number of songs about deserted love, and we girls always loved to sing them, but the boys were rather scornful of such songs. This is our family tune, and the words are the ones common in my part of the country, with the exception of the last verse which I began singing a long time ago, when my very first "truelove" took another girl to the pie supper!

I once did have a dear com-pan-ion,__ In-deed I thought his love my own,__ Un-til some black-eyed girl be-trayed me,__ And now he cares no more for me.

Last night you were so sweetly sleeping
And dreaming in some soft repose,
While I, a poor girl, broken-hearted
Was listening to the wind that blows.

I never did think of being without you,
I never could think of you a-being gone,
But all night long that wind keeps crying,
Farewell, truelove, I'm left alone.

Jubilee

Mom and Dad used to sing and play this party game when they were courting. It begins with boys and girls facing each other in two long lines, reel formation. On the first verse, hands are joined along the lines and at the ends to make a circle, and all circle left, once round until original place is reached. All drop hands and stand again in two lines, and at the be-ginning of the second verse and throughout the rest of the song, the head couple reels down to the bottom of the set while the others clap and sing. As soon as they reach the foot, the game starts over again with a new head couple.

S'all out on the old rail-road, All out on the sea, All out on the old rail-road, Far as I can see. Swing and turn, Ju-bi-lee, Live and learn, Ju-bi-lee.

Hardest work I ever done,
Working on the farm,
Easiest work I ever done,
Swing my true love's arm.
    (Swing and turn, etc.)

Coffee grows on a white oak tree,
Sugar runs in brandy,
Girls as sweet as a lump of gold,
Boys as sweet as candy.
    (Swing and turn, etc.)

Some will come on Saturday night,
Some will come on Sunday,
And if you give them half a chance
They'll be back a-Monday.
    (Swing and turn, etc.)

Saddle up the old gray horse,
Who will be the rider?
Ride him down to the old still house
And get a jug of cider.

If I had a needle and thread
As fine as I could sew
I'd sew my true love to my side
And down this creek I'd go.

In some lady's fine brick house,
In some lady's garden,
Let me out or I'll break out,
Fare ye well my darlin'.

If I had no horse to ride
I'd be found a-crawlin'
Up and down this rocky road
Lookin' for my darlin'.

I won't have no widder man,
Neither will my cousin,
You can get such stuff as that
Fifteen cents a dozen.

Wisht I had a big fine horse,
Corn to feed him on,
Pretty little girl to stay at home,
And feed him when I'm gone.

Sweet William and Lady Margaret

Mr. Begley was high sheriff of Perry County for several years. He used to be a familiar figure during campaign time, at various schoolhouse porches and local gathering places in the small villages throughout the hills, singing and playing his banjo. He made up many of his campaign songs, and could also sing for hours and never exhaust his store of old songs and ballads that the people loved to hear. It is said in our county that he was elected as a singer more than as a sheriff. After I was married, I took my new husband George Pickow around to meet some of my people, and we called on Justus and his family, and they all sang for us. This particular ballad he especially wanted to do for us because, years ago, when John and Alan Lomax had recorded his singing for the Library of Congress, he had sung them this song and had left out a verse. After he had sung it into my microphone, he felt that he had set the record straight.

As sung by Justus Begley, Hazard, Ky.

Sweet William a-rose one May morn-ing, And he dressed him-self in blue, We want you to tell us some-thing a-bout that long love be-tween La-dy Mar-g'ret and you. Well I know noth-in' a-bout Miss La-dy Mar-g'ret's love, And I know that she don't love me, But to-mor-row morn-in' at eight o'-clock, La-dy Mar-g'ret my bride shall see, But to-mor-row morn-in' at eight o'-clock La-dy Mar-g'ret my bride shall see.

Lady Margaret was standing in her own
  hall door
A-combing down her hair,
When who should she spy but Sweet
  William and his bride
And the lawyers a-riding by.
Well, she threw down her ivory comb,
Bound her hair in silk,
And she's stepped out of her own hall
  door
To never return any more.
And she's stepped out of her own hall
  door
To never return any more.

Well the day being past and the night
  a-coming on
When most all men was asleep,
Sweet William espied Miss Lady
  Margaret's ghost
A-standing at his own bed feet.
O it's how do you like your bed, she
  asked him,
And it's how do you like your sheet?
And it's how do you like that pretty
  fair miss
That's a-lying in your arms so sweet?
  (Repeat last two lines)

(Sung to last half of tune):
Very well, very well do I like my bed,
Very well do I like my sheet,
But the best one of all is that pretty
  fair miss
That's a-standing at my own bed feet.
  (Repeat last two lines)

Well the night a-being past and the day
  coming on
When most all men was at work,
Sweet William he said he was troubled
  in his head
From a dream that he dreamed last
  night.
Such dreams, such dreams they are
  no good,
Such dreams they are no good;
For I dreamt my hall was a-filled with
  wild swine
And my truelove a-swimming in blood.
  (Repeat last two lines)

He called his merry men to his side,
He counted one, two, three.
And the last one of them, go ask of my
  bride,
Lady Margaret I might go and see.
He rode till he came to Miss Lady
  Margaret's hall,
He pulled all on the ring,
No one was so ready as Lady Margaret's
  brother
To rise and welcome him in.

O is she in her garden, he asked him,
Or is she in her hall?
Or is she in the upper parlor
Amongst her ladies all?
She neither is in her garden, he
  answered,
She neither is in her hall,
But yonder she lies in her cold coffin
That's a-sitting by the side of the wall.

Hold up, hold up those milk white sheets,
That's made of linen so fine;
Tonight they shall hang o'er my Lady
  Margaret's corpse
And tomorrow they shall hang over
  mine.
Fold down, fold down those milk white
  sheets,
Made of silk so fine,
May I go and kiss those clay cold lips?
For they oftentimes have kissed mine.

Well first he kissed her on her cheek
And then he kissed her chin,
And then he kissed her clay cold lips
Which crushed his heart within.
Lady Margaret was buried in the new
  church yard,
Sweet William was buried close by her,
And out of her grave there sprang a
  red rose,
And out of his a briar.

(Sung to last half of tune):
They grew and they grew to the new
  church top.
Till they couldn't grow any higher,
Then they wound and they tied in a
  truelover's knot
For all truelovers to admire.

The Cuckoo

My family has always known this song, it seems. It is fairly similar to the variants found in and around Hindman in Knott County, where my father's folks lived. It is one of the saddest and loveliest songs I know.

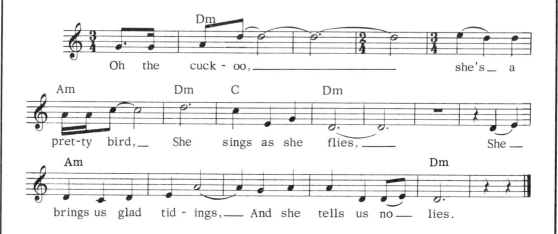

Oh the cuck - oo, _____ she's _ a pret-ty bird, _ She sings as she flies, _____ She _ brings us glad tid - ings, _ And she tells us no _ lies.

She sucks all pretty flowers
To make her voice clear,
And she never sings "cuckoo"
Till the spring of the year.

Come all you young women,
Take warning by me;
Never place your affection
On the love of a man.
For the roots they will wither,
The branches decay,
He'll turn his back on you
And walk square away.

If you do forsake me
I'll not be forsworn,
And they'll all be mistaken
If they think that I'll mourn,
For I'll get myself up in
Some higher degree
And I'll walk as light by him
As he can by me.

Old Betty Larkin

"Old Betty Larkin" is more of a young children's game than "Goin to Boston," which was a favorite of the courting age young people. But all ages joined in games like "Betty Larkin" at the Saturday night plays to which whole families went, baby-sitters not having come into fashion yet. Young and old could enjoy the partner-stealing, the skipping, the laughing good time they all had when this game was played. I remember one favorite aunt, a sister of Mom Ritchie's, who dearly loved to play the games, and as she got older and older she prided herself ever more on being able to outlast the young girls and boys on the floor. She often invited the neighbors to her house for the games, and I recollect more than one time when "Old Betty Larkin" began with one of her frisky young nephews grabbing Aunt Annie's hands and whirling her onto the floor, shouting, "Hop around, skip around, Old Betty Larkin!" Aunt Annie would whoop and laugh loud enough to be heard clear to the head of the holler, "Who you callin old?" I can out-skip you any time you say!" and the game would be on.

© 1940 by Geordie Music Publishing, Inc.

Hop a-round, Skip a-round, Old Bet-ty Lar-kin, Hop a-round, Skip a-round, Old Bet-ty Lar-kin, Hop a-round, Skip a-round, Old Bet-ty Lar-kin, Al-so my dear dar-lin'.

Steal, steal, old Betty Larkin,
Steal, steal, old Betty Larkin,
Steal, steal, old Betty Larkin,
Also my dear darlin'.

You take mine, and I'll take another,
You take mine, and I'll take another,
You take mine, and I'll take another
Also my dear darlin'.

Needles in a haystack, old Betty Larkin,
Needles in a haystack, old Betty Larkin,
Needles in a haystack, old Betty Larkin
Also my dear darlin'.

Hop around, skip around, old Betty
  Larkin,
Hop around, skip around, old Betty
  Larkin,
Hop around, skip around, old Betty
  Larkin,
Also my dear darlin'.

Lord Lovel

This song is almost as well-known and loved as is Barbara Allen, in our part of the country. Most of the tunes are lively, and almost dancy. In fact, it is only recently that I heard Jeannie Robertson in Scotland sing it slow and stately, the way Uncle Jason sang it in Kentucky. In this fast-moving world, the dancy tune is bound to be the one that appeals to most people, but if you have an easy mind and a lot of dishes to wash, or a stubborn baby to rock to sleep, here's our slow tune, which is after all more suited to the sadness of the story.

Where are you going, Lord Lovel, she said,
Oh where are you going, said she.
I'm going, my Lady Nancybell,
Strange countries for to see,
  - to see,
    Strange countries for to see.

When will you come back, Lord Lovel,
  she said,
Oh when will you come back, said she.
In a year or two or three at the most
I'll return to my fair Nancy, -Nancy,
  I'll return to my fair Nancy.

But he hadn't been gone a year and a
  day,
Strange countries for to see,
When languishing thoughts came into
  his head,
Lady Nancybell he'd go see, -go see,
  Lady Nancybell he'd go see.

So he rode and he rode on his milk-
  white steed
Till he came to London town,
And there he heard those parish
  bells ring
And the people go mournin' around,
  -around,
    And the people go mournin' around.

Oh what is the matter, Lord Lovel he
  said,
Oh what is the matter, said he.
A lord's lady's dead, a woman
  she said,
And some call her Lady Nancy, -Nancy,
  And some call her Lady Nancy.

He ordered the grave to be opened
  wide
And the shroud he turned down,
And there he kissed her clay cold lips
Till the tears came tricklin' down,
  -lin' down,
    Till the tears came tricklin' down.

Lady Nancy she died as it might be
today,
Lord Lovel he died as tomorrow;
Lady Nancy she died out of pure,
pure grief,
Lord Lovel he died out of sorrow,
of sorrow,
Lord Lovel he died out of sorrow.

Lady Nancy was laid in St. Francise's
Church,
Lord Lovel was laid in the choir,
And out of her bosom there grew a red
rose,
And out of her lover's a briar, -a
briar,
And out of her lover's a briar.

They grew and they grew to the church
steeple-top,
And then they could grow no higher,
So there they entwined in a true
lover's knot
For all true lovers to admire,
-admire,
For all true lovers to admire.

Fair and Tender Ladies

"The sad ones are the lovelye-est," old people have often said to me. This old love lament is about the best example of this statement that I know. The way I sing it is very near to the way I learned it from Uncle Jason, but he was getting on in years when he sang this one for me, and he was not too sure of the tune, singing it a bit differently on each verse, and forgetting a line of the words here and there. I have had to use my imagination in some spots, and supply words in others, so this resulting song is my way of singing "Fair and Tender."

Very freely sung a capella

Come all you fair and tender la - dies, take a warn-in' how you court young men, They're like a bright star on a cloud-y morn - ing, They'll first ap - pear and then they're gone.

They'll tell to you some loving story,
Make you believe their love is true.
Straightaway they'll go and court some other
And that is the love they have for you.

If I had a-known before I courted
That love had a-been such a killing thing,
I'd a-locked my heart in a box of golden
And a-fastened it up with a silver pin.

I wish I was some little sparrow,
That I had wings and I could fly.
I would fly away to my false truelover,
And while they'ed talk I'd sit and cry.

But I am not no little sparrow,
I have no wings and I can't fly;
I'll sit right here in my grief and sorrow
And pass my troubles by and by.

Young man, ne'er cast your eye on beauty,
For beauty is a thing that will decay;
I've seen many a fair and bright sunny morning
Turn into a dark and deludinous day.

Goin' to Boston

Many of the play-party games were simple, with the main object the choosing or trading of partners, or kissing, or tug-o-war; others had really complicated figures which looked for all the world like the forbidden set-dance steps (but of course they weren't, there being no fiddle nor any other stringed instrument of the Devil), and consequently were much more fun to do. "Boston" is at the top of every play-partners' list, having one of the finest tunes combined with the best of the running-set figures. I have always wondered, but haven't yet found anyone who can tell me for sure, whether the "Boston" in the song refers to the city in Massachusetts or the little town of Boston in England.

Saddle up, girls, and let's go with 'em,
Saddle up, girls, and let's go with 'em,
Saddle up, girls, and let's go with 'em
Ear-lye in the morning.

Out of the way, you'll get run over,
Out of the way, you'll get run over,
Out of the way, you'll get run over
Ear-lye in the morning.

Rights and lefts will make it better,
etc...

Swing your partner all the way to
Boston, etc...

Johnny, Johnny, gonna tell your Pappy,
etc...

Skin and Bones

"Skin and Bones" is a song with which we young'uns used to scare one another. We liked it best when there was someone in the room who hadn't heard it before; all of us would jump with fright and surprise at the end, no matter how many times we'd sung it before, but that person would jump the highest and holler the loudest. We always loved to sing it, even if just the family was there whenever we told ha'nt tales around the fireplace on winter evenings.

There was an old wo-man all skin and bones. Oo-oo-oo-oo—

One night she thought
She'd take a walk--
 Oo-oo-oooh!
She walked down by
The old graveyard--
 Ooo-oo-oooh!

She saw the bones
A-layin' around--
 Oo-oo-oooh!
She thought she'd sweep
The old church-house--
 Oo-oo-oooh!

She went to the closet
To get her a broom--
 Oo-oo-oooh!
She opened the door
And
 BOO!

The Old Woman and the Pig

"There was an Old Woman and She Had a Little Pig," to give its full title, is one of the first songs I learned to sing, since it is a wonderful baby-rocking song. It was such a family favorite that two of my sisters, after having been asked to sing at our oldest sister's wedding, stood prettily under the snowball bush in our yard and shouted out the whole tragic tale, to the embarrassment of the rest of the family and the great entertainment of the wedding guests.

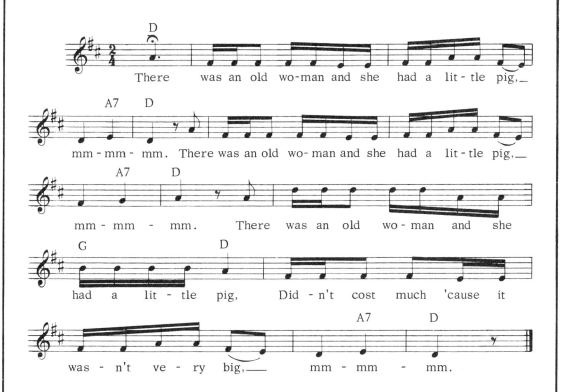

There was an old wo-man and she had a lit-tle pig, — mm-mm-mm. There was an old wo-man and she had a lit-tle pig, — mm-mm-mm. There was an old wo-man and she had a lit-tle pig, Did-n't cost much 'cause it was-n't ve-ry big, — mm-mm-mm.

Now this old woman kept the pig in the barn,
Mm-mm-mm.
Now this old woman kept the pig in the barn,
Mm-mm-mm.
Now this old woman kept the pig in the barn,
Prettiest little thing she had on the farm.
Mm-mm-mm.

Now this old woman fed the pig on clover,
It laid down and died all over.

The little piggy died cause it couldn't get its breath,
Wasn't that an awful death?

The little old woman she died of grief;
Wasn't that a sad relief?

The little old man he sobbed and sighed;
Then he too laid down and died.

Well, that was the end of the one, two, three,
Man and the woman and the little pig-ee.

The good old book lies on the shelf,
If you want any more you can sing it yourself.

The Turkish Lady

"...Uncle Jason went over to the corner of the porch to the well, drew up a fresh bucket of water and handed me a dipperful.

'Set and rest a minute now, and while you're a cooling off, maybe I can think of a song to sing you.'

I drank deep of the cold water while Uncle Jason sat and stared at the top-most mountain ridge across the holler. He began to tap his foot and hum, then to sing softly under his breath, 'Lord Bateman was a noble lord, he thought himself of a high degree,' and by the end of the second verse he was singing out loud and clear on the ballad of the Turkish Lady. Pretty soon I joined in too, for he sang the song with almost the same words and tune that we know at home." Reprinted from, Singing Family of the Cumberlands, Oak Publications.

A capella

Lord_ Bate-man was _ a no-ble lord, He thought him-self of a high de-gree, He could not rest nor be con-ten-ted, Till_ he had sailed_ the old salt_ sea.

Oh, he sailed east and he sailed to
  the westward,
He sailed all over to the Turkish
  shore,
There he got caught and put in prison
Never to be released any more.

There grew a tree inside of this
  prison
There grew a tree both broad and high,
And there they took and bound him
  prisoner
Till he grew weak and like to die.

Now the Turk he had one only daughter
And she was fair as she could be,
She stole the keys to her father's
  prison
And declared Lord Bateman she'd set
  free.

She took him down to the deepest
  cellar,
She gave him a drink of the strongest
  wine;
She threw her loving little arms
  around him,
Crying, Oh Lord Bateman, if you were
  mine.

They made a vow, they made a promise,
For seven long years they made it to
  stand;
He vowed he'd marry no other woman,
She vowed she'd marry no other man.

Well, seven long years has rolled
  around,
Seven years and they seem like
  twenty-nine;
It's she's packed up all of her gay
  clothing
And declared Lord Bateman she'd go
  find.

Well, she sailed east and she sailed to
  the westward,
She sailed all over to the England
  shore;
She rode till she came to Lord
  Bateman's castle
And she summonsed his porter right
  down to the door.

Oh, is this not Lord Bateman's castle,
And is his Lordship not within?
Oh yes, oh yes, cried the proud
  young porter,
He's a-just now bringing his new
  bride in.

Go bid him to send me a slice of bread,
Go bid him to send me a drink of wine,
And not to forget the Turkish lady
That freed him from his close confine.

What's the news, what's the news, you
  proud young porter,
What's the news, what's the news, that
  you brung to me?
There stands a lady outside of your
  castle,
She's the fairest one I ever did see.

She has got a gold ring on every finger,
And on one finger she has got three,
And enough gay gold all around her
  middle
As would buy Northumberland of thee.

She bids you to send her a slice of
  bread,
She bids you to send her a drink of
  wine,
And not to forget the Turkish lady
That freed you from your close confine.

Oh, up and spoke that new bride's
  mother,
She never was known to speak so
  free,
Well, what's to become of my only
  daughter,
She has just been made a bride to
  thee.

Oh, I've done no harm to your only
  daughter,
And she is the none of the worse for
  me;
She came to me with a horse and
  saddle
And she shall go home in coacharee.

Lord Bateman he pounded his fist on
  the table,
And he broke it in pieces one, two,
  three,
Says, I'll forsake all for the
  Turkish Lady,
She has crossed that old salt sea
  for me.

Oh, Love Is Teasin'

When I came to New York City in the Henry Street Settlement, one of the first friends I made in that place was Peggy Staunton, a lovely Irish girl who served delicious three-minute eggs with great decorum in our rather formal dining room. One day I followed her into the kitchen and found her lilting a beautiful Irish air and executing a perfect set of jig-steps between the great stove and the serving counter! In no time we were swapping songs and dance steps, and among countless other lovely songs Peggy sang this enchanting version of "Waly, Waly."

© 1953 by BMI

Slowly and freely

Oh, love is teas - in' and love is pleas - in' and love's a plea-sure when first it is new. But as love grows old - er it still grows cold er, and fades a - way like the morn-ing dew.

Come all ye fair maids, now take a
   warnin',
Don't never heed what a young man say.
He is like a star on some foggy mornin'
When you think he's near, he is far away.

I left my father, I left my mother,
I left my brothers and sisters too.
I left my home and my fond dwellin',
My dear young man, for the sake of you.

O love is teasin' and love is pleasin'
And love's a pleasure when first it is
   new,
But as love grows older it grows the
   colder
And fades away like the mornin' dew.

The Little Devils

The great English folksong collector, Cecil Sharp, told us that he had long heard in England how the "Farmer's Curst Wife" song used to have a whistled refrain, but he could find it nowhere existing in England. He was very happy and excited when my sister Una and our cousin Sabrina Ritchie sang and whistled it for him in Knott County, as they had learnt it from Sabrina's father, Uncle Jason Ritchie. Uncle Jason had to specialize in this song at play-parties around the countryside, because the young courting couples, when the singing would begin at resting times, liked to have "a funny one to settle down with."

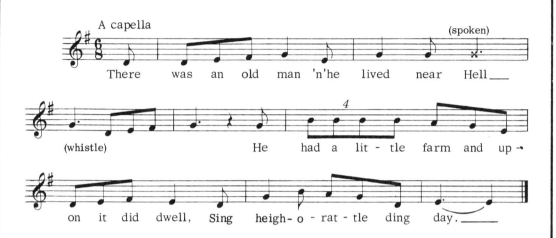

There was an old man 'n'he lived near Hell___ (spoken)
(whistle) He had a lit-tle farm and up-on it did dwell, Sing heigh- o - rat-tle ding day._____

O, the devil came to him one day at his plow,
There's one in your family I have to have now.

O it's neither your son nor your daughter I crave;
It's your old scolding wife and it's her I must have.

So he hobbst her up all on his back
And like a bold peddlar went packing his pack.

As they drew near the high gates of Hell,
Says, Rake back the coals boys and we'll roast her well.

Well, two little devils came a-rattling their chains;
She hauled back her cudgel and knocked out their brains.

Two more little devils peeped over the door;
She hauled back her cudgel, killed ninety-nine more.

Two more little devils peeped over the wall,
Sayin', Take her back Daddy, or she'll kill us all!

So he hobbst her up all on his back
And like a bold peddlar went packing her back.

Here's your old scolding wife and it's her I won't have;
She ain't fit fer Heaven, she shan't stay in Hell!

O, it's twenty years going and twenty coming back.
She called for the baccer she left in the crack.

O the women they are so much better than men;
When they go to Hell, they are sent back again.

25

What'll I Do With the Baby-O

In England, Scotland and Ireland, it is common for dance tunes, commonly played on the pipes or the fiddle, to have words put to them by generations of mothers and grannies, to bounce the baby by. The same is true in Kentucky, and I can remember when some of the verses to "Baby-O" must have been composed. During the work (corn-cultivation and harvesting) season, the young people would gather almost every Saturday night at someone's house to run sets. Set-running is like square dancing except that a set is not limited to four couples but is for "as many as will." Our whole family used to go, babes and all, and of course, along about ten-thirty at night,

we little ones would drop one by one around the room and be carried into the back room and placed on a big featherbed. There we lay, piles of babies, some sleeping, some whining, some yelling, and the mothers and big sisters would take turns staying with us, bouncing the bed up and down and singing ditty words to whatever tune was being fiddled in the next room. They'd try to think of funny things to make us laugh or keep us from crying. When I grew up, I had to take my own turn at bouncing that bed, and some of these words I made up myself!

What-'ll I do with the ba-by-o? What-'ll I do with the ba-by-o? What-'ll I do with the ba-by-o, If he don't go to sleep-y-o? Wrap him up in ca-li-co, Wrap him up in ca-li-co, Wrap him up in ca-li-co, Send him to his mam-my, o.

What'll I do with the baby-o,
What'll I do with the baby-o,
What'll I do with the baby-o
If he won't go to sleepy-o?
  Wrap him up in a tablecloth,
  Wrap him up in a tablecloth,
  Wrap him up in a tablecloth,
  Throw him up in the fodder-loft.

What'll I do, etc...
  Tell your daddy when he comes home,
  Tell your daddy when he comes home,
  Tell your daddy when he comes home,
  And I'll give Old Blue your chicken
    bone.

What'll I do, etc...
  Pull his toes, tickle his chin,
  Pull his toes, tickle his chin,
  Pull his toes, tickle his chin,
  Roll him up in the countypin. *

What'll I do, etc...
  Dance him north, dance him south,
  Dance him north, dance him south,
  Dance him north, dance him south,
  Pour a little moonshine in his mouth.

*Countypin--counterpane

What'll I do, etc...
Everytime the baby cries,
Stick my finger in the baby's eye!
That's what I'll do with the baby-o,
That's what I'll do with the baby-o.

The Hangman Song

According to the notes on Child ballad number 95, in English and Scottish Popular Ballads, the earliest known versions of this song have a girl as the victim, the song having apparently originated as, "The Maid Freed From the Gallows." It concerned a young woman who fell into the hands of corsairs, and each member of her family in turn refuses to pay ransom; then her lover comes and pays down the required fee. In our family variant as in most others from America and England,

it is (more properly!) a man who is being hanged, for what reason the song does not say. Aside from this change and the omission of motive, the story line is the same, the true love showing up on cue "for to take you home so we can married be." Mom always said that, "Well, if you're not particular, that's one way to get a husband"!

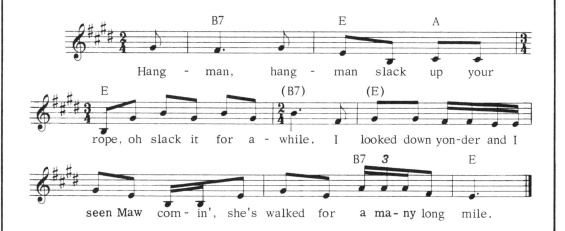

Hang - man, hang - man slack up your rope, oh slack it for a - while. I looked down yon-der and I seen Maw com - in', she's walked for a ma- ny long mile.

Hangman, hangman, slack up your rope,
O slack it for awhile.
I looked down yonder and I seen Paw
a-coming,
He's walked for a-many long mile.
    O Paw, say Paw, have you brung me
    any gold,
    Any gold to pay my fee?
    Or have you walked these many long
    miles
    See me on the hangin'-tree?
No son, no son, ain't brung you no gold,
No gold to pay your fee,
But I just walked these many long miles
See you on the hangin'-tree.

Hangman, hangman, slack up your rope,
O slack it for awhile.
I looked down yonder and I seen my
truelove coming,
She's walked for a-many long mile.
    O truelove, say truelove, have you
    brung me any gold,
    Any gold to pay my fee?
    Or have you walked these many long
    miles,
    See me on the hangin'-tree?
Yes love, truelove, I brung you some
gold,
Some gold to pay your fee,
And I just come for to take you home
So we can married be!

There Was A Pig Went Out to Dig

If this little song has any deep meanings, I don't know, though some claim that it has. I first heard it one summer at the John C. Campbell Folk School in Brasstown, N.C. It was printed in Songs of All Time, a fine collection of folk songs published by the Cooperative Recreation Service of Delaware, Ohio. That summer, "There Was a Pig" became everyone's favorite, and we were all making up verses...I'm sure that is the way the song was born in the first place, a gay chant started in an immortal happy moment of time by a child, or for a child, and added to and cherished by children of all ages, ever since.

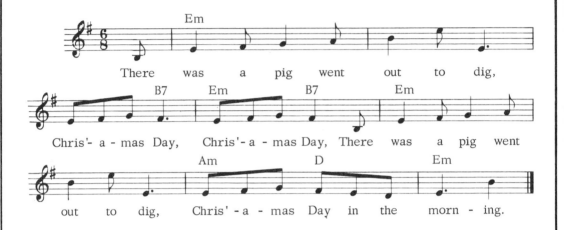

There was a pig went out to dig, Chris'-a-mas Day, Chris'-a-mas Day, There was a pig went out to dig, Chris'-a-mas Day in the morn-ing.

There was a cow went out to plough,
Christmas Day, Christmas Day,
There was a cow went out to plough,
On Christmas Day in the morning.

There was a sparrow went out to
harrow. . . .

There was a drake went out to
rake. . . .

There was a crow went out to
sow. . . .

There was a sheep went out to
reap. . . .

There was a minnow went out to
winnow. . . .

Golden Ring Around Susan Girl

I first heard and played this game when I was about six years old, in our little schoolyard in Viper, Kentucky. One day in spring, when school was out for dinner, a little girl named Hazel got some of us together and showed us how to play "Susan Girl." When I went home singing the song, my sisters Edna and Patty remembered additional verses to it, from their childhood on the schoolground. I have sung it through the years and taught it to Pete and Jonathan, and what the song is now is a combination of Hazel's and my sisters' words, and some of my own (because my memory of when I was six is not too clear). I suppose I have altered Hazel's tune, too, over this span of time, although I don't aim to apologize for that. Before folks learned to write music down, they had to depend upon their memories to get the tunes right. Also, in singing over and remembering them, it was just natural to adjust both tune and words to their own voices and singing styles. I am one of these musically illiterate folks, so, if someone will write out the tune for me, here is my "Susan Girl."

© 1963 by Geordie Music Publishing, Inc.

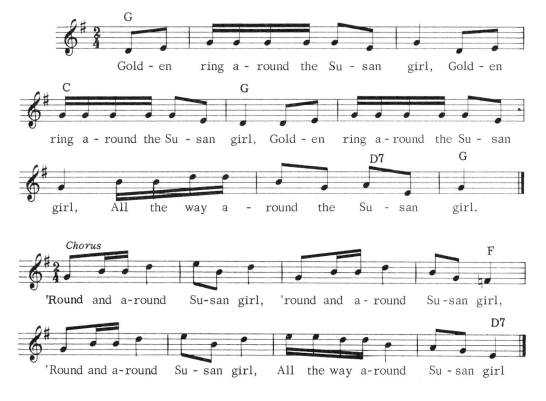

Golden ring around the Susan girl,
Golden ring around the Susan girl,
Golden ring around the Susan girl,
All the way around the Susan girl.

Take a little girl and give 'er a whirl,
Take a little girl and give 'er a whirl,
Take a little girl and give 'er a whirl,
All the way around the Susan girl.

Chorus: Round and a-round, Susan girl,
    Round and a-round, Susan girl,
    Round and a-round, Susan girl,
    All the way round, Susan girl.

Do-si-do left, Susan girl,
Do-si-do left, Susan girl,
Do-si-do left, Susan girl,
All the way around the Susan girl.

And do-si-do right, Susan girl,
Do-si-do right, Susan girl,
Do-si-do right, Susan girl,
All the way around the Susan girl.

Chorus: Round and round.... etc.

Rights and lefts, you Susan girl,
Rights and lefts, you Susan girl,
Rights and lefts, you Susan girl,
All the way around the Susan girl.

All run away with the Susan girl,
All run away with the Susan girl,
All run away with the Susan girl,
All the way around, Susan girl.

Chorus:

The Lyttle Musgrave

"We walked on, Uncle Jason talking slow and steady...'Now what song of all the ones I sung you today did you like the best? That one about the Lyttle Musgrave? It is a pretty thing, the language of it, and the dainty music. Reason I asked you is, I aim to sing your best liking for a parting.' Whereupon he stood very straight, put one hand on my shoulder...and sang. The little branch water sang along in a sweet dulcimer drone, like its music was made just in tune for the ballad.

Uncle Jason's tall, black-clad frame swayed to the quavery ups and downs of the song and his eyes clouded over with memories. He sang the whole song, all twenty-seven verses of it, and I don't have to tell you that I was black dark getting home." Reprinted from <u>Singing Family of the Cumberlands</u>, Oak Publications.

(Note: The spelling of "lyttle" is Uncle Jason's)

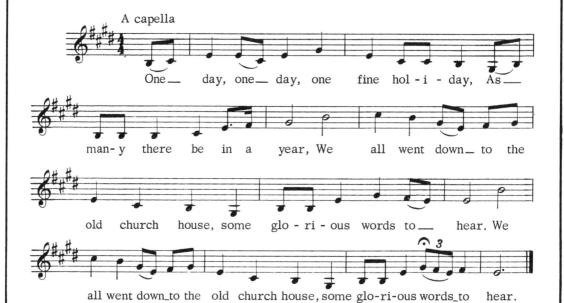

One day, one day, one fine hol-i-day, As man-y there be in a year, We all went down to the old church house, some glo-ri-ous words to hear. We all went down to the old church house, some glo-ri-ous words to hear.

Little Musgrave stood by the old
  church door,
The priest was at private mass,
But he had more mind of the fair
  women
Than he had for Our Lady's grace.
  But etc.

The first come in was a-clad in green,
The next was a-clad in pall,
And then come in Lord Arnol's wife,
She's the fairest one of them all,
  And then etc.

She cast her eye on Little Musgrave,
As bright as the summer sun,
And then bethought this little Musgrave,
This lady's heart have I won,
  On then etc.

Quoth she, I have loved thee, Little
  Musgrave,
Full long and many a day.
Quoth he, I have loved you, fair lady,
Yet never one word durst I say,
  Quoth he etc.

I have a bower at the Bucklesfordberry,
It's dainty and it's nice,
If you'll go in a-thither, my little
  Musgrave,
You can sleep in my arms all night,
  If you etc.

I cannot go in a-thither, said little
  Musgrave,
I cannot for my life,
For I know by the rings on your little
  fingers,
You are Lord Arnol's wife,
  For I etc.

But if I am Lord Arnol's wife,
Lord Arnol he is not home,
He is gone unto the academie
Some language for to learn,
   He is etc.

Quoth he, I thank you, fair lady,
For this kindness you show to me,
And whether it be to my weal or my woe
This night I will lodge with thee,
   And whether etc.

All this was heard by a little footpage,
By his lady's coach as he ran,
Says he, I am my lady's footpage,
I will be Lord Arnol's man,
   Says he etc.

Then he cast off his hose and shoes,
Set down his feet and he run,
And where the bridges were broken
   down,
He smote his breast and he swum,
   And where etc.

Awake, awake now, Lord Arnol,
As thou art a man of life,
Little Musgrave is at the Bucklesford-
   berry
Along with thy wedded wife,
   Little Musgrave etc.

If this be true, my little footpage,
This thing thou tellest to me,
Then all the land in the Bucklesford-
   berry
I freely will give it to thee,
   Then all etc.

But if it be a lie, thou little
   footpage,
This thing thou tellest to me,
On the highest tree in the Bucklesford-
   berry
It's a-hanged thou shalt be
   On the etc.

He called up his merry men all,
Come saddle to me my steed,
This night I am away to the Buckles-
   fordberry
For I never had greater need
   This night etc.

Some men they whistled and some they
   sung,
And some of them did say,
Whenever Lord Arnol's horn doth blow,
Away, Musgrave, away,
   Whenever Lord etc.

I think I hear the noisey cock,
I think I hear the jay,
I think I hear Lord Arnol's horn:
Away, Musgrave, away,
   I think etc.

Lie still, lie still, my little
   Musgrave,
Lie still with me till morn,
Tis but my father's shepherd boy
A-callin' his sheep with his horn,
   It is my etc.

He hugged her up all in his arms
And soon they fell asleep,
And when they awoke at ear-lie dawn
Lord Arnol stood at the bedfeet,
   And when etc.

Oh how do you like my coverlid,
Oh how do you like my sheet?
Oh how do you like my fair lady
Who lies in your arms so sweet,
   Oh how etc.

Oh I like your handsome coverlid,
Likewise your silken sheet,
But best of all your fair lady
Who lies in my arms so sweet,
   But best etc.

Arise, arise now, Little Musgrave,
And dress soon as you can;
It shall not be said in my countree
I killed a naked man,
   It shall etc.

I cannot arise, said Little Musgrave,
I cannot for my life,
For you have got two broadswords by
   your side
And I have got nary a knife,
   For you've etc.

I have two swords down by my side,
They both ring sweet and clear,
You take the best, I'll keep the
    worst,
Let's end this matter here,
    You take etc.

The first stroke that Little Musgrave
    struck,
He wounded Lord Arnol full sore;
The first stroke that Lord Arnol
    struck
Musgrave lay dead in his gore,
    The first etc.

Then up and spoke this fair lady,
In bed where as she lay,
Although you are dead, my little
    Musgrave,
Yet for your sake will I pray,
    Although you etc.

Lord Arnol stepped up to the bedside
Whereon these lovers had lain,
He took his sword in his right hand
And split her head in twain,
    He took etc.

Down Came An Angel

This Easter ballad is one of the most beautiful and moving in my family repertoire. The country folk in fashioning this song have given the members of the Holy Family the feelings, actions and speech of real people, and it is this human thing that reaches out of the song to touch our hearts. My father, it seems, had known the song when he was a young boy growing up on Clear Creek in Knott Co., Ky., the county adjoining Perry where he later moved, but he had not thought of it in years, until one weekend my sister Jewel came home singing it, and then he remembered. Jewel was teaching her first school there on Clear Creek and every morning one little boy kept hollering out, "Le's sing, 'Down Came an Angel!'" Jewel didn't know the song, but finally one morning she said, "All rignt, but you'll have to lead it." So he began it, and it turned out that the other students knew it too, and Jewel learned it from them and brought it home and re-taught it to us. Cecil Sharp (English Folk Songs From the Southern Appalachians) gives a North Carolina version, and Evelyn K. Wells (The Ballad Tree) gives the variant she learned from Edna Feltner in Pine Mountain, Ky. Although it is not often found in this country, I encountered it a few years ago in New York! I sang my version at a Country Dance Society party, and one of the members, Mrs. Baker, told me that she remembered the miners' wives singing it in a little different way from mine, as they went caroling from house to house in Wigan, England, when she was a girl.

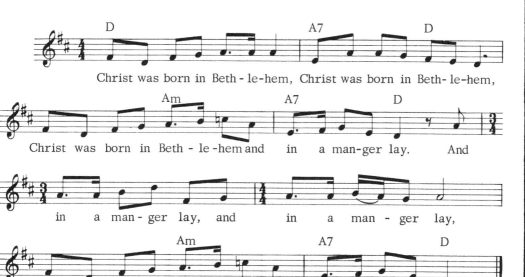

Christ was born in Beth - le-hem, Christ was born in Beth- le-hem,
Christ was born in Beth - le -hem and in a man-ger lay. And
in a man - ger lay, and in a man - ger lay,
Christ was born in Beth - le -hem and in a man - ger lay.

Judas, he betrayed him (3)
They nailed Him to the tree.

Joseph begged his body
And laid it in the tomb.

The tomb it would not hold him;
He burst the bands of death.

Down came an angel,
And rolled the stone away.

Mary, she came weeping
Her blessed Lord to see.

What's the matter, Mary?
They stole my Lord away.

Go and tell your brethren
He's risen from the dead.

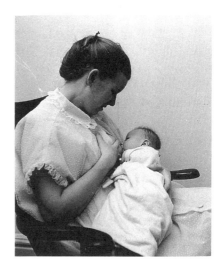

Among the Little White Daisies

This game-song is widely known throughout the South. A circle of children revolves about a child in the center during the first two verses. The center child names a sweetheart, and the line then changes directions and revolves the other way for two stanzas. For stanza five, everyone rests his head on his hands (pretending to be dead). In stanza six, everyone cries in sorrow for the widow (or widower). At the end of the last stanza, children in the circle kneel and the one center child, the "widow," counts heads round the circle to twenty-four, and the twenty-fourth child is "it" for the next round.

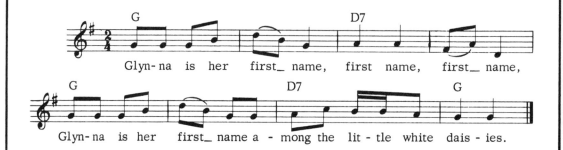

Glyn-na is her first name, first name, first name,
Glyn-na is her first name a - mong the lit - tle white dais - ies.

Combs is her second name,
Second name, second name,
Combs is her second name,
Among the little white daisies.

Pete is his first name,
First name, first name,
Pete is his first name,
Among the little white daisies.

Ritchie is his second name,
Second name, second name,
Ritchie is his second name,
Among the little white daisies.

Now poor Pete is dead and gone,
Dead and gone, dead and gone,
Now poor Pete is dead and gone
Among the little white daisies.

Left poor Glynna a widow now,
Widow now, widow now;
Left poor Glynna a widow now
Among the little white daisies.

Twenty-four children at her feet,
At her feet, at her feet,
Twenty-four children at her feet
Among the little white daisies.

(Count in rhythm 1 through 24.)

Bachelor's Hall

"That song is funny if you like to cry when you laugh," a long-married uncle of mine once observed, and his wife solemnly agreed with him. For both man and woman can feel that this is their song--it is almost as though the sexes are "answering-back" each other as the verses unfold. The woman begins the complaint, but in the last verse the man tells his troubles, and for once gets the last word.

©1963 by Stormking Music, Inc.

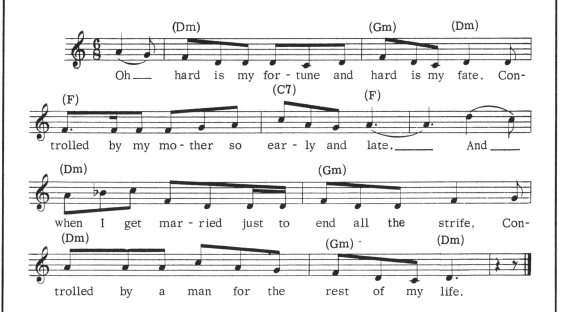

Oh— hard is my for-tune and hard is my fate. Con-trolled by my mo-ther so ear-ly and late.— And— when I get mar-ried just to end all the strife, Con-trolled by a man for the rest of my life.

O, young men go a-courtin' they dress
  up so fine,
They cheat the girls up, that is all
  their design;
They'll titter, they'll tatter, they'll
  laugh and they'll lie,
They'll cheat the girls up till they're
  ready to die.

When young men go a-courtin' they stay
  up all night,
Get out in the mornin' and look like a
  fright;
They saddle their horses, they rock
  and they reel,
Dag-gone them old girls, how sleepy
  I do feel!

O, bachelor's hall it is bound to be best,
Get drunk or stay sober, lay down take
  your rest,
No woman to scold you, no children to
  bawl,
So happy is the man that keeps
  bachelor's hall.

Carol of the Cherry Tree

I like Uncle Jason Ritchie's version of this song best, although we knew about three or four different ways to sing it in our house. I set it down here as near to his quavery style as I can get, with a few lines and quavers of my own to fill in the gaps in his memory. In Uncle Jason's words, "Now, have you ever heard that'n about Mary and Joseph and the argument over that cherry tree? Well that's a kind of a quare song, little story I guess never got printed in the Bible, but it got told by a whole lot of folks, and might be true, don't you know!"

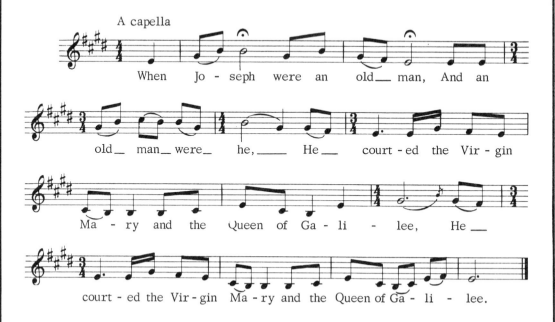

A capella

When Jo - seph were an old _ man, And an old _ man _ were _ he, _ He _ court - ed the Vir - gin Ma - ry and the Queen of Ga - li - lee, He _ court - ed the Vir - gin Ma - ry and the Queen of Ga - li - lee.

Joseph and Mary
Out a-walkin one day.
Here is apples and cherries
So fair to behold;
Here is apples and cherries
So fair to behold.

Mary spoke to Joseph,
And so softly spoke she:
O go and gather me some cherries
For I am with child;
O go and gather me some cherries
For I am with child.

Joseph flew in angry,
And in angry flew he,
Said Let the father of the baby
Gather cherries for you;
Said Let the father of the baby
Gather cherries for you.

Then up spoke Lord Jesus
From His Mother's womb:
Said, Bow low, low, cherry-tree;
Bow you low down to the ground.
Said, Bow low, low, cherry-tree,
Bow you low down to the ground.

The cherry tree bowed a-low down,
Low down to the ground,
And Mary gathered cherries
While Joseph stood around.
And Mary gathered cherries
While Joseph stood around.

Then Joseph took Mary
All on his right knee,
Said, Lord a-mercy on me
For what have I done?
Said, Lord a-mercy on me,
For I've slighted God's Son.

Then answered Lord Jesus,
Dear Joseph, make no moan;
Although you are the first to slight me,
You will not be alone;
Although you are the first to slight me,
You will not be alone.

Then Joseph took Mary
All on his left knee,
Said, Tell me, pretty Baby,
When your birthday shall be;
Said, Tell me, pretty Baby
When Your birthday shall be?

On the sixth day of January
My birthday shall be,
When the stars and the elements
Shall tremble with glee;
When the stars and the elements
Shall tremble with glee.

Shady Grove

"Once...Dad remembered for us...he was a little slip of a boy, about nine years old, and he was going to school to old man Nick Gerhart. They got through reciting their lessons and were all humming through their study, when Maggard Ritchie came in.

" 'He'd been off somewheres, courting in Virginny, and he had brought a feller home with him, and they'd come down to the schoolhouse to visit with Nick. Nick told the scholars to study away while he talked with the men, and for us not to look up. But you know that stranger had a fiddle in his hand, first one any of us had seen, and pretty soon he propped her up in the cradle of his arm here and commenced to play that thing. Lordie! I thought that was the prettiest sweepingest music. I hadn't heard a sound like that in my life before me, and it seemed like the only thing I'd been a-waiting for all this time... you could hear feet a-stomping all over the house, benches

a-screaking, younguns a-giggling, and nobody a-studying fit for a dog.

" 'Finally I let out a yell and lept off'n that bench and commenced to dance and clog around. Everybody hollered out a-laughing, and some of the other chaps jumped up, too. Teacher didn't even try to hold us, he was grinning and patting, too...the man played that tune over and over...after awhile they left, and Nick tried to settle us, put us back to our books, but I couldn't even see the print in that speller. I kept seeing that old fiddle bow race around on 'Shady Grove.' We around there had allus sung that tune middling fast, hopped around to it a little bit, but that fiddle had tuck out with that'n like the Devil was after her. I was so tickled about that, I kept laughing and wiggling around in my seat, and saying the words to 'Shady Grove' out loud instead of my lesson.' "
©1952 by Geordie Music Publishing, Inc.

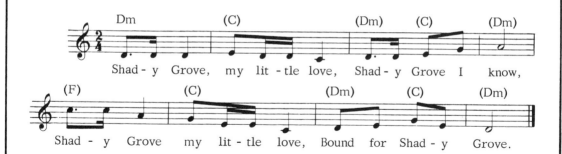

Shad - y Grove, my lit - tle love, Shad - y Grove I know,
Shad - y Grove my lit - tle love, Bound for Shad - y Grove.

Shady Grove, my little love,
Shady Grove I know;
Shady Grove, my little love,
Bound for the Shady Grove.

Cheeks as red as the blooming rose,
Eyes of the deepest brown;
You are the darling of my heart,
Stay till the sun goes down.

Shady Grove, my little love,
Shady Grove, I know;
Shady Grove, my little love,
Bound for the Shady Grove.

Went to see my Shady Grove,
She was standing in the door,
Shoes and stockings in her hand,
Little bare feet on the floor.

Shady Grove, my little love,
Shady Grove I know;
Shady Grove, my little love,
Bound for the Shady Grove.

Wish I had a big fine horse,
Corn to feed him on,
Pretty little girl, stay at home,
Feed him when I'm gone.

Shady Grove, my little love,
Shady Grove I know;
Shady Grove, my little love,
Bound for the Shady Grove.

Shady Grove, my little love,
Shady Grove I say,
Shady Grove, my little love
Don't wait till the Judgment day!

God Bless the Moonshiners

My sister Una is the one I most remember singing this song. Mom always frowned upon the singing by us girls of what she called "low" songs. Boys could sing them if they wanted to, and pick the banjer too, but a girl who thought anything of herself should not do either one. Una never sang this before Mom as I know of, but she told me that she learned it by walking up and down the creek (Clear Creek in Knott County, where the family lived then) with the other girls, on Sunday afternoons after church let out and dinner was over. The boys would be sitting on the store porch and steps picking banjers and dulcimers and singing boys' songs--murder ballads and rambling songs and things--and the girls would walk by and wave; they wouldn't think of stopping and joining the boys. They'd walk on down the creek, and the air would be so still they could hear every word just as plain, for a mile at least. She said the girls around there learned many a forbidden song this way. This one and "Little Cory" are two of them that she learned to sing in her own way and passed on to me.

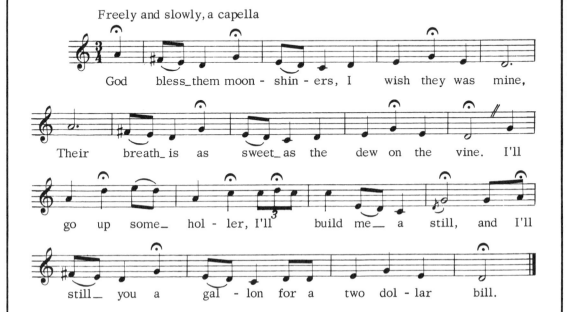

Freely and slowly, a capella

God bless_them moon - shin - ers, I wish they was mine, Their breath_ is as sweet_ as the dew on the vine. I'll go up some_ hol - ler, I'll build me_ a still, and I'll still_ you a gal - lon for a two dol - lar bill.

I've been a moonshiner
For seventeen long years,
I've spent all my money
On whiskey and beer.
God bless the moonshiners,
I wish they was mine;
Their breath is as sweet as
The dew on the vine.

I'll go to the alehouse,
I'll drink with my friends.
No woman to follow
To see what I spend.
God bless the moonshiners,
I wish they was mine;
Their breath is as sweet as
The dew on the vine.

I'll eat when I'm hungry,
I'll drink when I'm dry;
Pretty women when I'm lonesome,
Sweet Heaven when I die.
God bless the moonshiners,
I wish they was mine;
Their breath is as sweet as
The dew on the vine.

Little Cory

Wake up, wake up lit - tle Co - ry, What_ makes you
sleep_ so _ sound? When the mar - shalls are a -
com - in', Gon - na tear your still - house_ down.

Go way, go way, little Cory,
Quit your hanging around my bed;
Bad likker has ruint my body,
Pretty women has gone to my head.

The last time I seen little Cory,
She was standing with a bottle in her
   hand,
A-drinkin' down her sorrows,
Cause they took away her man.

Don't you hear them bluebirds a-singin'?
Don't you hear that mournful sound?
Don't you hear them bluebirds a-singin'?
My truelove she lies under the ground.

Go dig me a hole in the meadow,
Go dig me a hole in the ground,
Go dig me a hole in the meadow,
For to lay little Cory down.

I ain't a-gonna work tomorrow;
I ain't a-gonna work next day.
I'll stay at home in sorrow,
If it is Christmas Day.

See the Waters A-Gliding

The old, old story of the soldier and the lady is told and retold, sung and resung, in almost as many different ways as is the tale of Barbara Allen or Lord Randal. At least three quite distinctive tunes exist in our mountain community. Here is my own, and my favorite, version. Being at present a great-aunt twenty-five times, I love the good moralizing final verse!

©1965 Geordie Music Publishing, Inc.

I bid you good-morning, good-morning
  to thee.
O where are you going, my pretty lady?
I'm going out walking for the joy of the
  Spring,
To see the waters a-gliding, hear the
  nightingales sing.

Chorus:
See the waters a-gliding,
Feel the joys of the Spring,
See the waters a-gliding,
Hear the nightingales sing.

Well a-walking and a-talking for an
  hour or two.
Then out from his knapsack a fiddle he
  drew,
And the tune that he played made the
  whole mountain ring,
O listen, O listen, how the
  nightingales sing!

And now you pretty lady, it's time to
  go home.
O no, my dear soldier, play just one
  tune more,
For I'd rather hear your fiddle, or the
  touch of one string
Than to see the waters gliding, hear
  the nightingales sing.

O now my dear soldier, won't you marry me?
O no, my pretty lady, that never can be;
I've a wife down in London and children twice three;
Two wives and six children's too many for me.

I'll go back to london to bide there one year,
But it's every long day I'll remember my dear;
And if ever I come back, it will be in the Spring
To see the waters gliding, hear the nightingales sing.

So come all you young ladies, my warning to hear:
If you meet a brave soldier in the spring of the year,
Don't let him detain you, he wants just one thing;
To see the waters gliding, hear the nightingales sing.

The Holly Bears the Berry

I first heard this carol sung by Mrs. Raymond McLain at Berea, Kentucky. Much later, I found it in The Oxford Book of Carols under the title of "Sans Day Carol." The footnote to the song explains the title and gives the sources: "has been so named because the melody and the first three verses were taken down at Saint Day in the parish of Gwennap, Cornwall.

Saint Day (or They) was a Breton saint whose cult was widely spread in Armorican Cornwall. We owe the carol to the kindness of the Rev. G.H. Doble, to whom Mr. W. D. Watson sang it after hearing an old man, Mr. Thomas Beard, sing it at Saint Day."

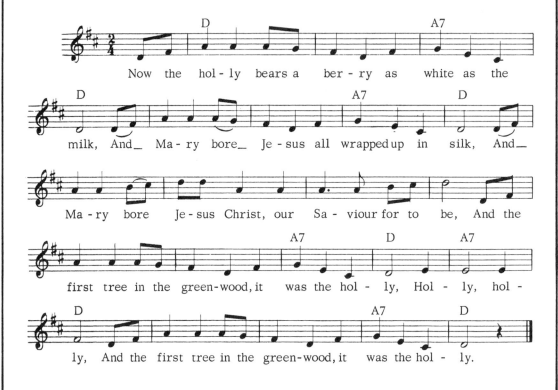

Now the hol-ly bears a ber-ry as white as the milk, And_ Ma-ry bore_ Je-sus all wrapped up in silk, And_ Ma-ry bore Je-sus Christ, our Sa-viour for to be, And the first tree in the green-wood, it was the hol-ly, Hol-ly, hol-ly, And the first tree in the green-wood, it was the hol-ly.

Now the Holly bears a berry as red as the blood,
And Mary bore Jesus, to do us all good. (Chorus)

Now the Holly bears a berry as black as the coal,
And Mary bore Jesus, who died for us all. (Chorus)

I Saw Three Ships

In our family, this carol is associated with my sister Patty. I remember her singing it about the housework when I was very little. She and the other girls who were lucky enough to go away to high school at Pine Mountain probably learned it there and brought it home. We have sung it, together as a family and apart in our many different homes now (as we have married and started new families) over a period of many years. If each of us has made as free with the song as I have, in taking it to our hearts and singing it to our children, there are probably twelve different versions of Patty's song, now, within the Ritchie family!

I saw three_ ships come_ sail - int in on _ Christ - mas Day,_ on _ Christ - mas Day. I saw three_ ships come_ sail - ing in on_ Christ-mas Day_in _ the morn-ing. And_what was in those_ ships all three, on_ Christ - mas Day_ on_ Christ - mas Day, And_ what was in those_ships all three, on_ Christ-mas Day_ in _ the morn-ing.

The Mother Mary and her Baby,
  On Christmas Day, on Christmas
    Day;
The Mother Mary and her Baby
  On Christmas Day in the morning.
He sat and smile-ed on her knee,
  On Christmas Day, on Christmas
    Day,
He sat and smile-ed on her knee
  On Christmas Day in the morning.

Bless-ed be God, likewise His Son
  On Christmas Day, on Christmas
    Day;
Bless-ed be God, likewise His Son
  On Christmas Day in the morning.
Thus did she sing the whole day long
  On Christmas Day, on Christmas
    Day;
Thus did she sing the whole day long
  On Christmas Day in the morning.

And all the bells on earth did ring
  On Christmas Day, on Christmas
    Day;
And all the bells on earth did ri ng
  On Christmas Day in the morning.
And all the angels in Heaven did sing
  On Christmas Day, on Christmas
    Day,
And all the angels in Heaven did sing
  On Christmas Day in the morning.

Father Get Ready

I once asked Mom Ritchie why the church songs were all so mournful, and she said, "Why, they sound more like worship and God than any other music I know." In her opinion, modern hymns are too dancy.

The Old Regular Baptists came into the Kentucky Mountains as circuit-riders, bringing the first organized religion up the dark hollers where, if you can believe my Aunt Mary Ritchie, shooting and moonshining was the only religion that the menfolks knew. No one has been able to tell me exactly where the Old Regular's style of singing comes from, although the music in the Wee Free Kirks in the Hebrides comes perhaps nearer to the sound than that of any other one region. In Kentucky, the song leader begins the song without announcement, often while the preacher is still winding up his sermon (sometimes it is a signal for him to remember to wind it up, putting-on of the brakes, calling the excited preacher back to this world and helping him to slow down and stop). This song leader sings the first line alone, then he calls or chants out the second line, and the congregation joins in. He lines out each line, on to the end of the song. This was probably done in the early days because of the scarcity of books, but it is still done today even though everybody knows all the songs by heart. Even now, the leader is still the only one to hold the book, usually the Sweet Songster, which has words only. Under each song title there is an indication as to what meter the song uses, and the leader chooses a fitting tune from among hundreds known by the worshippers.

I remember walking the two miles down the river road with Mom and Dad, on early solemn Sundays. We were always late, because the singing began as early as eight-thirty in the morning. The style was slow, stately and much decorated, each song having all its many verses sung. Many of the old members had walked or ridden (horseback) much further than we had, and everybody had been waiting for a whole month to join in the social singing of their favorites with their friends. Once a month was as often as the circuit-rider could get there to hold meeting in the old days; now the once-a-month meeting is simply a matter of tradition...Well, we would know that we were late, just before we rounded the Big Bottom Bend and came in sight of the white clapboards of the Little Zion Church, for we could then begin to hear, distant and indescribably beautiful, the singing, a sound filled with sadness and reverence, ancient modal tunes that rose and crashed with the majesty and immensity of great mountainous waves on the ocean.

© 1955 by Geordie Music Publishing, Inc.

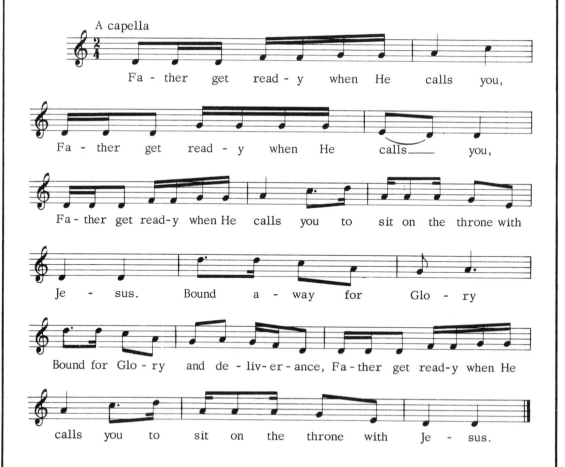

A capella

Fa - ther get read - y when He calls you,
Fa - ther get read - y when He calls___ you,
Fa - ther get read - y when He calls you to sit on the throne with Je - sus. Bound a - way for Glo - ry
Bound for Glo - ry and de - liv - er - ance, Fa - ther get read - y when He
calls you to sit on the throne with Je - sus.

Mother get ready when He calls you
Mother get ready when He calls you
Mother get ready when He calls you
To sit on the throne with Jesus.

    Bound away for Glory,
    Bound for Glory and deliverance,
    Mother get ready when He calls you
    To sit on the throne with Jesus.

This world is a trouble and sorrow,
World is a trouble and sorrow,
This world is a trouble and sorrow
The only bright light is Jesus.

    Bound away for Glory,
    Bound for Glory and deliverance,
    This world is a trouble and sorrow
    The only bright light is Jesus.

We'll all be happy in the morning
We'll all be happy in the morning
We'll all be happy in the morning
A-sitting on the throne with Jesus.

    Bound away for Glory,
    Bound for Glory and deliverance,
    We'll all be happy in the morning
    A-sitting on the throne with Jesus.

Amazing Grace

A capella

a - ma-zing grace_ how_ sweet the sound that saved a _ wretch like_ me.

I once was lost___ but_ now_ I'm found, was blind but now_ I see.

T'was grace that taught my heart to
    fear,
And grace that fear relieved.
How precious did that grace appear,
The hour I first believed.

Through many dangers, toils and snares,
I have already come.
T'was grace that brought me safe thus
    far,
And grace will lead me home.

    When we've been there ten thousand
        years,
    Bright shining as the sun.
    We've no less days to sing God's praise
    Than when we first begun.

The Day Is Past and Gone

We lay our garments by
Upon our beds to rest;
So Time will soon disrobe us all
Of what we now possess.

Lord, keep us safe this night,
Secure from all our fears.
May angels guard us while we sleep
Till morning light appears.

And when our days are past
And we from time remove,
O may we in Thy bosom rest,
The bosom of Thy love.

I've Got A Mother Gone to Glory

A capella

I've got a moth-er gone to Glo - ry, I've got a moth-er_ gone to Glo - ry, Look a-way_ o-ver yon-der on the Gold-en Shore. A - way up in Heav - en, A - way up in Heav - en. I've got a moth-er_ gone to Glo - ry, Look a-way_ o-ver yon-der on the Gold-en Shore.

Some bright day I'll go and see her,
Some bright day I'll go and see her,
Look away over yonder on the Golden
   Shore.

  Away up in Heaven
  Away up in Heaven,
Some bright day I'll go and see her,
Look away over yonder on the Golden
   Shore.

That bright day may be tomorrow,
That bright day may be tomorrow,
Look away over yonder on the Golden
   Shore.
  Away up in Heaven (as above)

(Same verses may be repeated for
  Father, Sister, Brother, etc.)

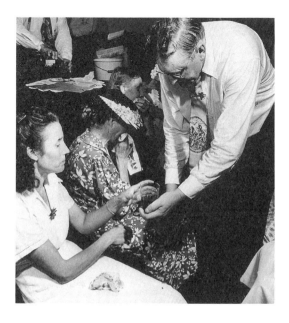

Guide Me, Oh Thou Great Jehovah

Slowly and freely a capella

Guide me ___ Oh ___ Thou ___ Great Je - ho - vah, ___
I am ___ weak ___ but ___ thou art ___ might-y, ___

Pil - grim through ___ this bar - ren ___ land.
Hold ___ me with ___ Thy pow'r - ful ___ hand.

Bread of ___ Heav - en feed me ___ 'til ___ I ___ want ___ no ___ more. ___

Bread ___ of ___ heav - ven, ___ Bread of ___ Heav - en

feed ___ me ___ 'til ___ I ___ want ___ no ___ more.

Open now the crystal fountains,
Whence the healing waters flow;
Let the fiery, cloudy pillar
Lead me all my journey through.
   Strong Deliv'rer,
   Be Thou still my strength and shield.
   Strong, Deliv'rer, strong Deliv'rer,
   Be Thou still my strength and shield.

When I tread the verge of Jordan,
Bid my anxious fears subside.
Bear me through the swelling current,
Land me safe on Canaan's side.
   Songs of praises I will ever give to
    Thee,
   Songs of praises, songs of praises
   I will ever give to Thee.

Twilight A-Stealing

Ever since our family grew large enough to enjoy evening sings together, this twilight hymn has been a favorite. Many people think, "Twilight A-Stealing" is a silly sentimental song; certainly it isn't a genuine folk song. Some say it is a hymn, but then it isn't really religious either. Whatever it is, it always expresses what we feel as a family, together, and it is our own happy home we think about when we sing, "Gleameth the mansion, filled with delight, sweet happy home so bright."

Twi-light a-steal-ing o-ver the sea,
Sha-dows a-fall-ing dark on the lea, Borne on the night wind,
voi-ces of yore, Come from the far-off shore.
Far-a-way be-yond the star-ry sky, Where the
love-light nev-er, nev-er dies, Gleam-eth a man-sion
filled with de-light, Sweet hap-py home so bright.

Voices of loved ones, songs of the past
Still linger round me, while life shall last,
Cheering my pathway, while here I roam,
Seeking my far-off home.

Come in the twilight, come, come to me,
Bringing sweet message over the sea;
Lonely I wander, sadly I roam,
Seeking my far-off home.

Lord Randal

I'm told that this old story of the young man who meets his doom by getting too mixed up with too many womenfolk is to be found all over Europe, even in Italy. I've heard many a different way of singing it myself, and if you look it up in Bronson's newly published Traditional Tunes to the Child Ballads, you will see how very well known and widespread it is, for he lists 103 known variants! The verses and the air I give here are Uncle Jason's, with a few words and phrases and turns of my own that have crept in, in adapting it to my voice and making it my song. What I like about this particular version is its straightforwardness and simplicity. The tune can be almost spoken, as a story is told rather than sung, taking away the temptation on the part of the singer to act it out with much beating of the breast that is so embarrassing to the folk song audience.

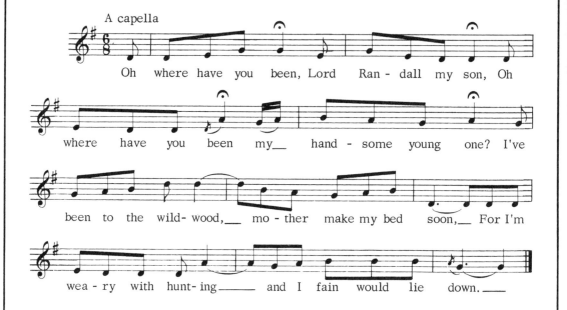

A capella

Oh where have you been, Lord Ran - dall my son, Oh where have you been my__ hand - some young one? I've been to the wild- wood,__ mo - ther make my bed soon,__ For I'm wea - ry with hunt - ing_____ and I fain would lie down.____

Where did you get dinner, Lord Randall
  my son,
Where did you get dinner, my handsome
  young man?
I dined with my true love, mother make
  my bed soon,
For I'm weary with hunting and I fain
  would lie down.

Oh what did she feed you, Lord Randall
  my son,
What did she feed you, my handsome
  young man?
I had eels boiled in broth, mother
  make my bed soon.
For I'm weary with hunting and I fain
  would lie down.

What's become of your bloodhounds,
  Lord Randall my son,
What's become of your bloodhounds,
  my handsome young man?
Oh they swelled and they died, mother
  make my bed soon,
For I'm weary with hunting and I fain
  would lie down.

Oh I fear you are poisoned, Lord
  Randall my son,
I fear you are poisoned, my handsome
  young man.
Oh yes I am poisoned, mother make my
  bed soon,
For I'm sick at my heart and I fain
  would lie down.

What will you leave your old father,
 Lord Randall my son,
What will you leave your old father, my
 handsome young man?
My castle and land, mother make my
 bed soon,
For I'm sick at my heart and I fain
 would lie down.

What'll you leave your old mother,
 Lord Randall my son,
What'll you leave your old mother, my
 handsome young man?
My gold and my silver, mother make
 my bed soon,
For I'm sick at my heart and I fain
 would lie down.

What'll you leave your own true love,
 Lord Randall my son,
What'll you leave your own true love,
 my handsome young man?
Oh I'll leave her hell fire, mother
 make my bed soon,
For it's now I am dying and I got to
 lie down.

Two Dukes A-Roving

This game-song is known, in some form or other, throughout the English-speaking world, and is played by children in many parts of the United States, usually on school play-yards. Boys join hands in one line, and girls in another, facing the boys. The boys march toward the girls, then back into place, singing the first verse. The girls advance and retire in like manner, answering with the second verse. This procedure is repeated until the choosing verse is reached, then the boy at the end of the line fills in the name of his choice when the boys sing, "The fairest one that I can see is, come along ____ and go with me." The boy then claims her and takes her over to his side, and she becomes his partner for the next game, after all the other boys have had their choices.
©1940 by Geordie Music Publishing, Inc.

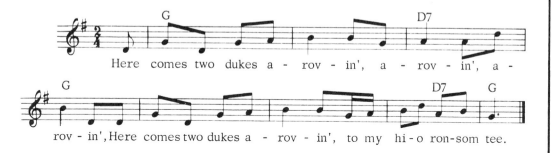

Here comes two dukes a - rov - in', a - rov - in', a -
rov - in', Here comes two dukes a - rov - in', to my hi - o ron-som tee.

Boys— Here comes two dukes a-roving,
 A-roving, a-roving;
 Here comes two dukes a-roving
 To my heigh-O ransom tee.

Girls— What is your good will Sir,
 Good will Sir, good will Sir?·
 What is your good will Sir?
 To my heigh-O ransom tee.

Boys— Our will it is to marry,
 To marry, to marry;
 Our will it is to marry,
 To my heigh-O ransom tee.

Girls— Will you have any one of us, Sir,
 Of us, Sir, of us, Sir?
 Will you have any one of us, Sir?
 To my heigh-O ransom tee.

Boys— You look too brown and drowsy,
 (Follow pattern above)

Girls— We're quite as fair as you are.

Boys— The fairest one that I can see,
 That I can see, that I can see,
 The fairest one that I can see
 Is come along, Sally, and go
 with me.

The May Day Carol

The Ritchies were singing 'The May Day Carol' before I was born, so it seems to me to have been always ours. My older sisters learned it while they were in school at Pine Mountain at the Settlement School there. It is English in origin, and so much like the other songs we know that Kitty, Patty, Edna and Jewel soon made it their own. The English custom on May Day is to go in a group about the village singing the May song (each locality has its own) and leaving fresh May greens and flowers over the door of each house. In Kentucky, we children used to make May baskets with flowers and greenery gathered in the woods, and we would leave them at our friends' doors, but we didn't dare linger to sing for fear we'd be recognized (and the fun was to guess who made each basket). So we sang the carol on any soft spring evening when the family and friends gathered to share good talk, stories and music. (Tradition Records TLP 1031)

I've been a-wan-drin' all the night, And the best part of the day, And when I turn back home a-gain, I will bring you a branch of May.

A branch of May I will bring you,
   my love,
Here at your door I stand;
It's nothing but a sprout, but it's well
   budded out
By the work of the Lord's own hand.

Take a Bible in your hand
And read a chapter through,
And when the Day of Judgement comes
The Lord will think on you.

In my pocket I hold a purse
Tied up with a silver string;
All that I need is a little silver
To line it well within.

My song is done and I must be gone,
I can no longer stay;
God bless you all, both great and small
And send you a joyful May.

Darby Ram

"'The Darby Ram" was Grandmother Hall's favorite lullaby song, my Mom would tell me, and that she could hear Grandmother singing it more than any other. Her given name was Patty, and she was gentle-natured and laughing, and had a beautiful face and a lot of wavy dark-brown hair. That's all Mom could remember of her, for she died early...when Mom was still 'little Abbie,' child enough to be rocked on her mother's lap, and smiled down on and sung to when she was sleepy or hurt. Abbie sang this song then with its bright memory to all her many babies, and the love and the remembering in her voice made it a very special song for all of us." Reprinted from <u>Singing Family of the Cumberlands</u>. J. Ritchie Oak Publications.

© 1955 by Geordie Music Publishing, Inc.

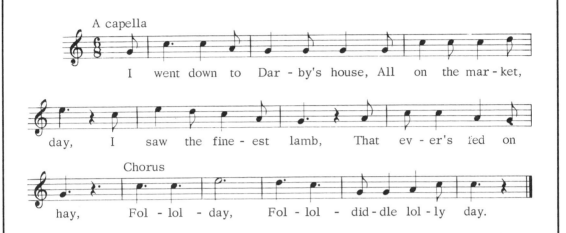

I went down to Dar - by's house, All on the mar - ket, day, I saw the fine - est lamb, That ev - er's fed on hay,

Chorus

Fol - lol - day, Fol - lol - did - dle lol - ly day.

The first tooth he had
Held a hundred of a horn,
The next tooth he had
Held sixty barrel o'corn.
Fol lol day, Fol lol diddle lolly day.

Four feet he had
Four feet stood on the ground,
And every foot he had
Covered a half an acre of ground.
Fol lol day, Fol lol diddle lolly day.

The wool on the ram's belly
Drug nine miles on the ground,
I went down to Darby's house
And stole a thousand pound.
Fol lol day, Fol lol diddle lolly day.

The wool on the ram's back
It reached up to the sky,
The eagles built their nests there,
You could hear the young uns cry.
Fol lol day, Fol lol diddle lolly day.

The one that cut his throat
Got drownded in the blood
The one that held his head
Got washed away in the flood.
Fol lol day, Fol lol diddle lolly day.

Little Bitty Baby
(Children Go Where I Send Thee)

We learned this song from Opal Payne, Hindman, Kentucky, "visiting game-teacher" to all the Knott County Schools. On one of her visits to the Breedings Creek Colored School, she found the children lined up, boys on one side of the room facing the girls on the other side, singing, "Children Go" in answer-back fashion. She took down the song and taught it to the folks at the Hindman Settlement School wnere she worked. Everyone loved it; it spread like a brushfire. Pauline, my sister who was at Hindman School then, brought it back to the rest of us.

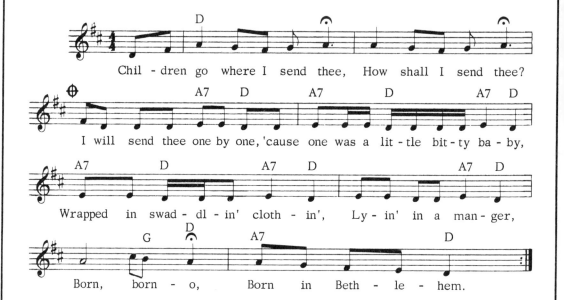

Chil - dren go where I send thee, How shall I send thee? I will send thee one by one, 'cause one was a lit - tle bit-ty ba - by, Wrapped in swad - dl - in' cloth - in', Ly - in' in a man - ger, Born, born - o, Born in Beth - le - hem.

Children go where I send thee,
How shall I send thee?
　I will send thee two by two,
　Cause two was the Paul and Silas,
　One was a little bitty baby
　Wrapped in swaddling clothing,
　Lying in a manger.
Born, born-o,
Born in Bethe-lye-hem.

Children go where I send thee;
How shall I send thee?
　I will send thee three by three
　Cause three was the three wise riders,
　Two was the Paul and Silas,
　One was (etc.)

Cause four was the four come a-knocking at the door.

Cause five was the guardian angels.

Cause six was the six that couldn't get fixed.

Cause seven was the seven went up to Heaven.

Cause eight was the eight that stood at the gate.

Cause nine was the nine got left behind.

Cause ten was the Ten Commandments.

Brightest and Best

"On Old Christmas Eve we'd sit fore the fire and Mom and Dad and Granny'd tell us about the baby Jesus born in a stable on this night, and they'd say that if we'd go out at midnight we'd see the elderberry bush blooming in the fence corner right in the snow, and that if we'd peep in through a chink in our stable and make no racket atall we'd see the cow and the old mule kneeling, paying honor to the little King of Kings. Then maybe Granny'd sing us her Christmas carol, 'Brightest and Best,' in the old mountain tune, and we'd all sing some...That used to be our Christmas. It was a good, peaceful kind of time...Now I guess everybody celebrates the Day this (new) way...but in the evening of the fifth day of January, I still always think on Granny Katty sitting bowed over the fire, singing of the little Babe with dewdrops a-shining on His cradle." Reprinted from, Singing Family of the Cumberlands, J. Ritchie–Oak Publications.

Hail the blest morn when the Great Me-di-a-tor, Down from the re-gions of Glo-ry des-cends. Shep-herds go wor-ship the Babe in the man-ger, Lo! for a guard the bright an-gels at-tend. Bright-est and best of the suns of the morn-ing, Dawn on our dark-ness and lend us thine aid; Star of the east the ho-ri-zon a-dorn-ing, Guide where our In-fant Re-deem-er is laid.

Cold on his cradle the dewdrops are shining,
Low lies His head with the beasts of the stall;
Angels adore Him in slumber reclining,
Maker and monarch and king of us all.
(Chorus)

Say, shall we yield Him in costly devotion
Odors of Edom and offerings divine?
Gems from the mountains and pearls from the ocean?
Gold from the forest and myrrh from the mine?
(Chorus)

Vainly we offer each ample oblation,
Vainly with gifts would His favor secure.
Richer by far is the heart's adoration,
Dearer to God are the prayers of the poor.
(Chorus)

Keep Your Garden Clean

Some few years ago, Miss Evelyn K. Wells asked me to learn this song and sing it onto a personal recording for her, to be used for her lecturing purposes. I got to liking it so well that I have been singing it ever since. It is an Ozark version of the English "Seeds of Love," and the tune is not unlike that of the Ritchie song, "The Time Draws Near."

©(from Randolph, Ozark Folksongs, I,357)

Come all you pret-ty fair_ maids,Who flou-rish in your prime,Be

sure to keep your gar-den clean, Let __ no one take your thyme.

My thyme it is all gone away,
I cannot plant anew;
And in the place where my thyme stood,
It's all growed up in rue.

Stand up, stand up you pretty hope,
Stand up and do not die;
And if your lover comes to you,
Pick up your wings and fly.

The pink it is a pretty flower,
But it will bud too soon;
I'll have a posy of my own,
I'm sure t'will wait till June.

In June comes in primrose flower,
But that is not for me;
I will pluck up my primrose flower
And plant a willow tree.

O willow, green willow
With sorrow mixed among,
To tell to all this wide world
I loved a false young man.

Bow Your Bend to Me

I learned this sad tale from my sister Una, when I was very young. In the family, we generally used the fast, dancy tune that is the most commonly known one around the country. Sung to this melody, the song makes the best illustration I know of the fact that, in the early days of musical mankind, song and dance were one--when a ballad was sung, it was also danced. However, as our family sings it, the story of the "two sisters" has been taken over by the tale-tellers around wintry hearths. The melody, slow, stately and free, gives singer and audience plenty of time to savor the tune and ruminate on the plot as the drama unfolds. There was never any hurry, on these evenings, and no vast audience demanding to be entertained or to clap along, so the singer or singers could be completely at ease. At one time we all sang these old ballads in unison, but since we have scattered abroad and haven't sung together in several years, we are amused and amazed to find that nowadays we twelve (two are gone) have twelve distinct sets of words and twelve slightly different melodies to everything! Here is my way.

© 1965 by Geordie Music Publishing, Inc.

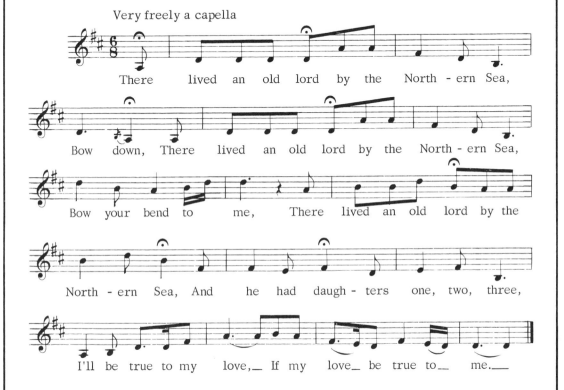

Very freely a capella

There lived an old lord by the North-ern Sea,
Bow down, There lived an old lord by the North-ern Sea,
Bow your bend to me, There lived an old lord by the North-ern Sea, And he had daugh-ters one, two, three,
I'll be true to my love,_ If my love_ be true to_ me._

A young man came a-courting there,
And he took his choice of the youngest fair.

He gave this youngest a beaver hat,
The oldest she thought little of that.

He gave this youngest a gay gold ring,
The oldest not one single thing.

Oh sister, oh sister, let's us walk out,
And see those little ships go sailing about.

As they walked down by the salty brim,
The oldest pushed that youngest in.

Oh sister, oh sister, lend me your hand,
And you shall have my dowry land.

I'll neither lend you my hand nor glove,
But I will have your own true love.

Oh down she sank and away she swam,
Into the miller's dam she ran.

He robbed her of her gay gold ring,
And then he pushed her in again.

The miller was hanged at his own mill-gate,
The oldest sister was burned at the stake.

The Unquiet Grave

This is Uncle Jason's version of "The Unquiet Grave." He would often recite the words, sadly and reverently, and when he came to the lines, "the fairest flower that ever grew is withered to a stalk," he would murmur almost to himself, "It's so true, so true!" At last one day I asked him whether he had a tune for this one, and he looked surprised and said, "Why, any number of tunes'll fit it. Just pick you out one."

I told him that I'd rather he did the choosing, and he finally sung it off for me, to the tune I give you here. It is I believe, a mixture of one-fourth Old Regular Baptist hymn-tune, and three-fourths his own invention. When he finished, he said with satisfaction. "There. I think that tune is pretty fair."

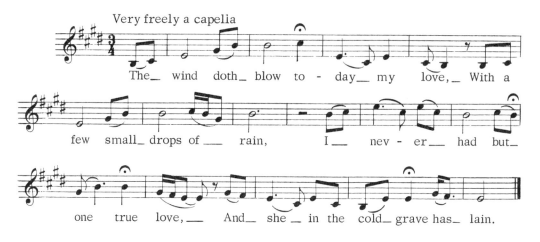

Very freely a capella

The_ wind doth_ blow to - day_ my love,_ With a few small_ drops of __ rain, I_ nev - er_ had but_ one true love, __ And_ she _ in the cold_ grave has_ lain.

I'll do as much for my truelove
As any young man may;
I'll sit and mourn all on her grave
For a twelvemonth and a day.

The twelvemonth and a day being up,
The dead began to speak:
Who is this mourns all on my grave
And will not let me sleep?

Tis I, my love, mourns on your grave
And will not let you sleep;
I crave one kiss from your clay-cold lips
And that is all I seek.

You crave one kiss from my clay-cold
    lips;
My breath is earthly strong.
If you had one kiss from my clad-cold
    lips,
Your time would not be long.

Go down in yonders garden green,
Love, where we used to walk.
The fairest flower that ever grew
Is withered to a stalk.

The stalk is withered dry, my love,
So must our hearts decay.
So make yourself content, my love,
Till God calls you away.

The Flower Carol

In my family, we have always loved "Good King Winceslas" sung to this tune, not knowing that any other tune existed. I was surprised, therefore, to read this note about "Wenceslas" in The Oxford Book of Carols: "This rather confused narrative owes its popularity to the delightful tune, which is that of a Spring carol, 'Tempus adest floridum,' No. 99 (from a rare Swedish book, Piae Cantiones--editor's note). Unfortunately, Neale (ed.note: the Reverend J. M. Neale) in 1853 substituted... this 'Good King Winceslas,' one of his less happy pieces, which E. Duncan goes so far as to call, 'doggeral,' and Bullen condemns as 'poor and commonplace to the last degree...'...we reprint the tune in its proper setting, not without hope that...

'Good King Winceslas' may gradually pass into disuse, and the tune restored to Springtime."

Now, over one hundred years since the legend of the Good King was first printed, it seems a forlorn hope on the part of the Oxford Book editors (may they rest in peace) that he will eventually die a natural death. I am, like the rest of the world, fond of 'Good King Winceslas,' but, having a bit of the purist in me and being ever the one to want to set matters straight, I choose to present here the original "Flower Carol." (Reprinted from album notes for "Carols of All Seasons," Tradition Records, TLP 1031)

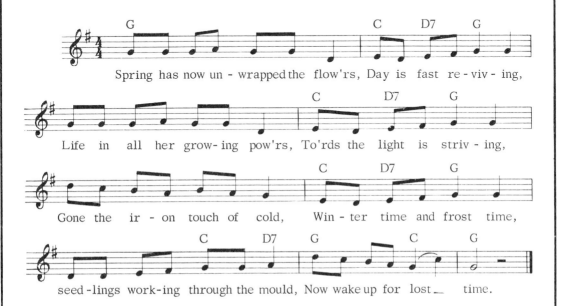

Spring has now un-wrapped the flow'rs, Day is fast re-viv-ing, Life in all her grow-ing pow'rs, To'rds the light is striv-ing, Gone the ir-on touch of cold, Win-ter time and frost time, seed-lings work-ing through the mould, Now wake up for lost time.

Herb and plant that, winter long,
Slumbered at their leisure,
Now bestirring, green and strong,
Find in growth their pleasure;
All the world with beauty fills
Gold and green enhancing,
Flowers make glee among the hills
And set the meadows dancing.

Earth puts on her dress of glee;
Flowers and grasses hide her.
We go forth in charity,
Brothers all beside her;
For, as man this glory sees
In the awakening season,
Reason learns the heart's decrees
And hearts are led by reason.

Praise the Maker, all ye saints,
He with glory girt you;
He who skies and meadows paints
Fashioned all your virtue;
Praise Him, seers, heroes, kings,
Heralds of perfection;
Brothers, praise Him, for He brings
All to resurrection!

Lord Thomas and Fair Ellender

"And then would come the time when my heavy eyelids began to droop, and my mind to wander all around and the people in the ballads would pass before me out there in the sparkly dusk...alive and beautiful. Fair Ellender rode slowly by on her snow-white horse, her hair like long strands of silver and her face like milk in the moonlight. Then came her waiting maids, dressed all in green and holding their heads high and proud...Lord Thomas, tall and brave with sword shining in his hand...the wedding folk around the long table. Then, in some easy manner that never had to be explained, I became Fair Ellender, and the movement of the porch swing became the slow, graceful walking of the white horse. Hundreds of people lined the broad highway as I rode by, taking me to be some queen, as the song wound its way to the tragic ending." <u>Singing Family of the Cumberlands</u>, Oak Publications ©1955 by Geordie Music Publishing, Inc.

A capella

Oh mo-ther, oh mo-ther come rid-dle it down,__ Come rid-dle two hearts_ as_ one, Say must I mar-ry fair El-len_ der, ___ Or bring the brown_ girl, _ home. The brown girl, she has houses and lands, fair El-len-der she_ has_ none, Oh the best ad-vice I can give you my_ son, ___ Is go bring me the brown_ girl_ home.

He rode till he come to fair Ellender's
  gate,
He tingled the bell with his cane,
No one so ready as fair Ellender
  herself
To arise and bid him come in.

  Oh what's the news, Lord Thomas,
    she cried,
  What's the news you brung to me,
  I've come to ask you to my wedding,
  Now what do you think of me?

Oh mother, oh mother, come riddle it
  down,
Come riddle two hearts as one,
Oh must I go to Lord Thomas's wedding
Or stay at home and mourn.

  Oh the brown girl she's got
    business there,
  You know you have got none;
  Oh the best advice I can give you,
    my daughter,
  Is to stay at home and mourn.

She dressed herself in a snow-white
   dress,
Her maids they dressed in green,
And every town that they rode through
They took her to be some queen.

   She rode till she come to Lord
     Thomas's gate,
   She pulled all in her rein;
   No one so ready as Lord Thomas
    himself
   To arise and bid her come in.

He took her by the lily-white hand,
He led her through the hall,
He seated her down in a rockin'-chair,
Amongst those ladies all.

   Is this your bride, Lord Thomas,
    she cried,
   She looks so wonderful brown,
   You once could-a married a maiden
    as fair
   As ever the sun shone on.

Dispraise her not, fair Ellender, he
   cried,
Dispraise her not to me,
For I think more of your little finger
Than of her whole body.

   The brown girl had a little pen
    knife,
   It being both keen and sharp,
   Betwixt the long ribs and the
    short,
   Pierced fair Ellender to the heart.

Oh what's the matter, Lord Thomas he
   cried,
You look so pale and wan,
You used to have a rosy a color
As ever the sun shone on.

   Oh are you blind, Lord Thomas,
    she cried,
   Or is it you cannot see;
   And can't you see my own heart's
    blood
   Come a-trinkling down to my knee,

Lord Thomas he drew his sword from
   his side,
As he run through the hall;
He cut off the head of his bonny
   brown bride
And kicked it against the wall.

   Then placin' the handle against
    the wall,
   And the blade a-towards his heart,
   Said, did you ever see three true-
    lovers meet
   That had so soon to part.

(Sung to second half of tune)

Oh mother, oh mother, go dig my grave,
And dig it both wide and deep,
And bury fair Ellender in my arms,
And the brown girl at my feet.

The Old Soap-Gourd

Mom Ritchie gave us this play-party game, remembered from her own childhood, and we adapted it to ours. In the song, the boys in the game are the "soap-gourds" and the girls are "lily-bushes." To play it, the children form a ring and walk around one boy who is "it," blindfolded in the center. At the end of the second verse, he points and the circle stops. The girl nearest to where he is pointing joins him in the center, and they swing, skipping around with a two-hand swing, while those in the circle clap hands for them. The boy then leaves the center and joins the outside circle, and the chosen girl remains as the "lily-bush" as the game continues.

Here we go 'round the old soap gourd, the old soap gourd, the old soap gourd, Here we go 'round the old soap gourd, ear - lye in the morn - in'.

The old soap-gourd likes sugar in his
   tea
And sometimes takes a little brandy,
Every time he turns around,
Chooses the girl comes handy.

Rise and give me your lily-white hands,
Swing me around so handy;
Rise and give me a love-lye kiss,
Sweet as sugar candy.

(If the one in the center is a girl, the song is the same except that she is called a "lily-bush" instead of "the old soap-gourd.")

Joe Bowers

"Uncle" Jason Ritchie's brother (Jason was really Dad's first cousin), back in the late 1800's, took a ramble through Arkansas, Missouri and Texas. From him and others like him who "went West" and returned, Kentucky Mountain folks learned several songs about gold rushes, cowboy life, etc., that have nothing to do with our own tradition. Other such "foreign" songs were learned during the Civil War when soldiers from all over the country camped together. Our family, with its nine redheads, especially enjoyed the joke at the end of "Joe Bowers," that, "Sally had a baby and the baby had red hair!"

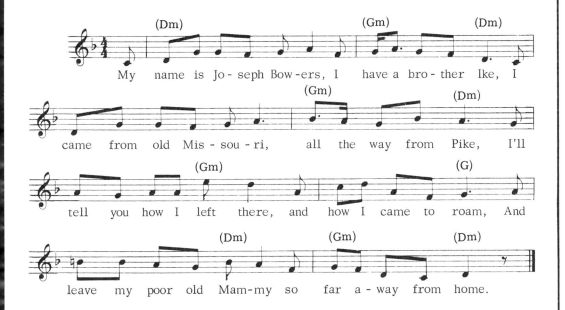

My name is Jo-seph Bow-ers, I have a bro-ther Ike, I came from old Mis-sou-ri, all the way from Pike, I'll tell you how I left there, and how I came to roam, And leave my poor old Mam-my so far a-way from home.

I used to court a girl there, her name
  was Sally Black.
I asked her if she'd marry me, she said
  it was a whack.
Says she to me, Joe Bowers, before
  we hitch fer life,
You ought to have a little home to take
  your little wife.

O Sally dear, O Sally, O Sally, for
  your sake,
I'll go to Californy and try to raise a
  stake.
When I got to that country, I hadn't
  nary a red,
And I had such wolfish feelings,
  I wisht myself most dead.

At length I went to mining, put in the
  biggest licks
Right down upon the boulders, just like
  a thousand bricks.
I worked both late and early, in rain
  and sun and snow,
I was working for my Sally, it was all
  the same to Joe.

At last I got a letter from my dear
  brother Ike,
It came from old Missouri, all the way
  from Pike.
It brought to me the darndest news that
  ever you did hear--
My heart is almost bursting, so pray
  excuse this tear.

It said that Sal was false to me, her
  love from me had fled;
She'd got married to a butcher and the
  butcher's hair was red;
And more than that, the letter said,
  t'was enough to make one swear--
That Sally had a baby, and the baby
  had red hair.

(Repeat tune of last two lines):
And whether twas a boy or girl, the
  letter never said,
It only said the baby's hair was inclined
  to be red!

Love Somebody, Yes I Do

This is a fiddle tune first, and a song second. I remember square dancing to the music all my young life. The words are but "ditties" or humorous fragments, thrown out by the fiddler sometimes in the midst of his playing. If, on the spur of the moment, he thought of a funny line of his own, he threw that in, too, to amuse the dancers.

©1965 by Geordie Music Publishing, Inc.

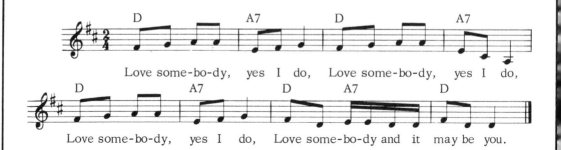

Love some-bo-dy, yes I do, Love some-bo-dy, yes I do,
Love some-bo-dy, yes I do, Love some-bo-dy and it may be you.

Twice sixteen's thirty-two,
Twice sixteen's thirty-two,
Twice sixteen's thirty-two,
Sally won't you have me? Do, gal, do!

Sun comes up and the moon goes down,
Sun comes up and the moon goes down,
Sun comes up and the moon goes down,
See my little Sally in her mornin' gown.

F'somebody come, find me gone,
Somebody come, find me gone,
F'somebody come, find me gone,
They better leave my girl alone!

Love somebody, sure and true,
Love somebody, sure and true,
Love somebody, sure and true,
Love somebody and a-maybe you.

Old Virginny

This beautiful family love song comes to me from my father, who used to slip off into the deep woods on Sundays with his young friends to play "forbidden music" on the homemade gourd fiddles. In that time, anything that wasn't church singing was sinful, and the fiddle was without question the instrument of the Devil. "Old Virginny" was one of the songs that was thus saved by my "sinful" father--sung and played softly in the hush of long-ago Sunday stillnesses. Thank God! But we have wondered many a time since then, how many other songs were lost forever?

©1953 by BMI

I was born in old Vir - gin-ny, to North Ca -ro-li - na I did go. I fell in love with a pret -ty fair mai - den, and her name I did not know.

Her hair was of some brightsome color,
Her cheeks were of a rosy red,
And in my heart I loved her dearly,
Many a tear for her I shed.

When I am asleep I'm a-dreaming about you,
When I am awake I find no rest;
And every moment seems like an hour
With aching pains all acrost my breast.

To my heart you are my darling,
At my door you're welcome in;
At my gate I'll meet you my darling,
O if your love I could only win.

I'd ruther be in some dark valley
Where that sun don't never shine,
Than to see you another man's darling
When I know that you should be mine.

When I am dead and in my coffin
And my feet's towards the sun,
Come and sit beside me darling,
Come and think on the ways you've done.

The Death of Cock Robin

The children from Mace's Creek, up the holler from Viper, used to sing this tune to "Cock Robin" at Friday afternoon programs in our little two-room school. After the last recess on Friday, the teacher couldn't get the students to study much anyway, so we usually took turns "reciting" or singing our special songs for the others. When I heard one I liked, I'd learn it from the singer at the next recess or on the way home. This was an easy tune to learn, being almost like the universal children's chant. I have forgotten who the two little girls were who sang it, on that long-ago Friday afternoon, but this is their tune, and some of their words, filled in with some family ones and a few of my own remembered from rocking-to-sleep days with my own little sons.

Who killed Cock Ro-bin? It was I, said the spar-row, with my lit-tle bow and ar-row, It was I, it was I, said the spar-row.

Who saw him die?
It was I, said the fly
With my little tiny eye,
It was I, it was I, said the fly.

Who caught his blood?
It was I, said the fish
With my little silver dish,
It was I, it was I, said the fish.

Who made his coffin?
It was I, said the snail
With my little hammer and nail,
It was I, it was I, said the snail.

Who sewed the shroud?
It was I, said the beetle,
With a little darnin' needle,
It was I, it was I, said the beetle.

Who dug his graven?
It was I, said the crow
With my little spade and hoe,
It was I, it was I, said the crow.

Who carried him to it?
It was I, said the boar,
With my little coach-and-four,
It was I, it was I, said the boar.

Who preached the funeral?
It was I, said the swaller
Just as loud as I could holler,
It was I, it was I, said the swaller.

Who tolled the bell?
It was I, said the bull
Just as hard as I could pull,
It was I, it was I, said the bull.

Who mourned his dyin'?
It was I, said the mole,
For the passing of his soul,
It was I, it was I, said the mole.

Bandyrowe

Here is one of our favorite lullabies, and one which lends itself to adding verses about those present at the time. The "John" and "Pete" in these verses are our two sons, Jonathan and Peter Pickow. The "kitty alone" refrain is often found attached to some version of the Frog's Courtship.

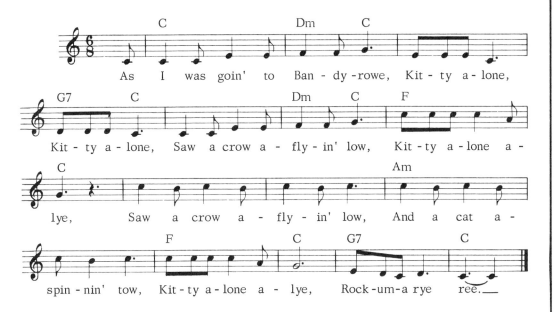

As I was goin' to Ban-dy-rowe, Kit-ty a-lone, Kit-ty a-lone, Saw a crow a-fly-in' low, Kit-ty a-lone a-lye, Saw a crow a-fly-in' low, And a cat a-spin-nin' tow, Kit-ty a-lone a-lye, Rock-um-a rye ree.

In came a little bee,
  Kitty alone, Kitty alone,
In came a little bee,
  Kitty alone a-lye,
In came a little bee
With his fiddle upon his knee.
  Kitty alone a-lye,
  Rock-a-ma-rye-ree.

Next came in was two small ants,
Fixin around to have a dance.

Next came in was little John,
One shoe off and one shoe on.

Next came in was little Pete,
Fixin' around to go to sleep.

As I was goin to Bandyrowe,
  Kitty alone, Kitty alone,
Singin' bye-O-baby-O,
  Kitty alone, a-lye,
As I was goin' to Bandyrowe
Singin' bye-O-baby-O,
  Kitty alone a-lye,
  Rock-a-ma-rye-ree.

Pretty Saro

When a person hears this song for the first time, he usually thinks, if he notices it at all, what a commonplace tune and what trite words. "Pretty Saro" is just that, there's no denying. All the same, the scoffer will soon find himself humming that commonplace tune and he will also discover that those trite words will not leave his mind and heart. It is one of the simplest, loveliest songs ever sung. We especially like to sing this one on the porch, along about the edge of dark, with all the high and low voices filling in the harmonies.

Down in some lone val-ley in a lone-some. place, Where the wild birds do whis-tle and their notes do in-crease, Fare-well Pret-ty Sa-ro, I bid you a-dieu, And I'll dream of Pret-ty Sa-ro where ev-er I go.

My love she won't have me, so I understand;
She wants a free-holder who owns house and land.
I cannot maintain her with silver and gold,
Nor buy all the fine things that a big house can hold.

If I were a merchant and could write a fine hand,
I'd write my love a letter that she'd understand;
I'd write it by the river where the waters o'erflow;
And I'll dream of pretty Saro wherever I go.

The Miracle of Usher's Well

Uncle Jason didn't sing this one for me until I had left home, finished college and come back for a visit. He said that it had been a-many a year since he had thought on it, much less sung it, but given a day or two he was able to recollect this much of it. It seems very complete in some parts, but doesn't have the verses at the end wherein the sons entreat the mother not to cry any more over their graves, as her tears wet their winding-sheets. According to authorities on the subject, these winding-sheet verses are only found in American versions of the ballad, never in the older Scottish or English variants. It would seem, then, that Uncle Jason's "Miracle of Usher's Well" has been preserved almost unchanged from a Scottish source. I had to fit a tune to it, as he could not remember much of a one, saying in his usual offhand way, "O, there's several that will go to that one." When, later on, I sang it for him in the tune I had fashioned, he said, "Why, shore, that suits it fine. I do believe that's the right one, now."

Very freely a capella

There lived a wife — at — Ush - er's_ Well, And a weal - thy wife___ was_ she, She had three_ strong and stal - wart_ sons, And she sent_ them o'er ___ the ___ sea.

They hadn't been gone but a week from her,
But a week and only one;
When word was sent to this wealthy wife
That her sons were dead and gone.

They hadn't been gone three weeks from her,
Three weeks and only three,
When word was sent to this wealthy wife
That her sons she'd never see.

She prayed the wind would never cease,
Nor troubles in the flood,
Till her three sons came home to her
In their own flesh and blood.

It fell about the Martinmas time,
When nights are long and dark,
This wife's three sons came home to her
With robes all shining bright.

Blow up the fire my maidens fair,
Bring waters from the well,
For we shall have a merry, merry feast
Since my three sons are well.

Oh it's she has made for them a bed,
She made it large and wide,
And placed her mantle over them all
And sat down at their side.

The cock he chaffed his wings and crowed
Before the break of day;
The eldest to the youngest said:
It's time we were a-way.

The cock doth crow, the day doth dawn,
The merry birds doth chide,
We shall be missed out of our place
And we must no longer bide.

Lie still, lie still, but a little while,
Lie still but if we may,
If our mother misses us when she wakes up
She'll go mad e'er the break of day.

So fare ye well my mother dear,
For we must say goodbye
And fare thee well the bonny lass
That kindles my mother's fire.

Gentle Fair Jenny

The men in the family always favored this one, for reasons easy to see. I don't see that there's anything so funny about a man whupping his wife, although I do admit that this Gentle Fair Jenny maybe needed a tap or two. To appreciate why, you have to understand that in the Kentucky Mountains, the womenfolk used to have to (some still do!) do all the work about the house, tending the stock, milking, raising the children, in addition to being field hands and often doing the plowing as well. The men hunted, claimed they were bringing meat to the table. Knowing this, you can understand that if a man married a woman who wouldn't even cook the vittles, that would be a natural catastrophe.

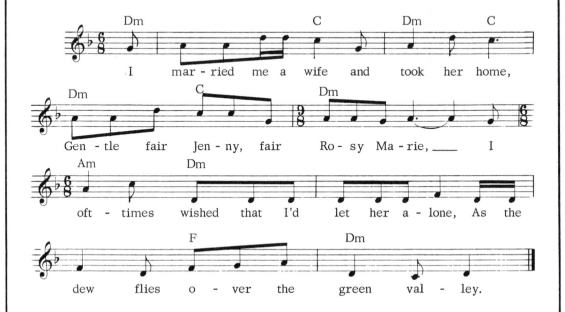

I mar-ried me a wife and took her home, Gen-tle fair Jen-ny, fair Ro-sy Ma-rie, ___ I oft-times wished that I'd let her a-lone, As the dew flies o-ver the green val-ley.

All in my kitchen she would not use,
For fear of spoiling her new cloth shoes.

First day at noon I come in from the plow,
My dearest wife is my dinner ready now?

There's a little piece of corn bread layin' on the shelf,
If you want anymore you can cook it yourself

Second day at noon I come in from the plow,
My dearest wife, is my dinner ready now?

Get out of here you dirty thief,
If you want any dinner you can cook it yourself.

I got my knife and went out to the barn,
I cut me a hickory as long as my arm.

I took my limb and I went back,
Around her back I made it crack.

I'll tell my father and all of my kin,
You whupped me with a hickory limb.

You can tell your father and all your kin
I whupped you once and I'll whup you again.

I Wonder When I Shall Be Married

Our family had its worries. There were eleven girls born in our house, and only three boys, and that seemed to be pretty much the pattern all through the community. This little song the girls used to sing over the dishwashing, and by the time the older ones got up into their teens, it had come to have real meaning. By the time I came along, it was well established in our locality as "the Ritchie old-maid song."

© 1946 by Geordie Music Publishing, Inc.

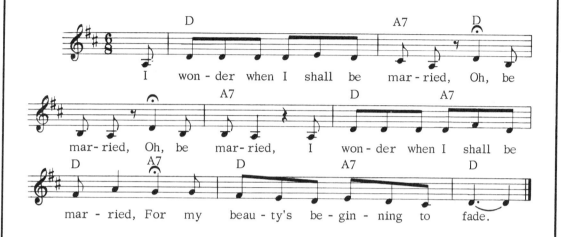

I won - der when I shall be mar - ried, Oh, be mar - ried, Oh, be mar - ried, I won - der when I shall be mar - ried, For my beau - ty's be - gin - ning to fade.

My mother she is so willing, Oh, so
willing, . . .
My mother she is so willing for she's
four daughters besides.

My father has forty good shillings . . .
and they will be mine when he dies.

My shoes have gone to be mended. . .
and my petticoat's gone to dye green.

And they will be ready by Sunday . . .
Oh, say! Won't I look like a queen?

A cup, a spoon, and a trencher . . . and
a candlestick made out of clay.

Oh, say! Won't I be a bargain . . . for
someone to carry away?

I wonder when I shall be married, Oh,
be married, Oh, be married;
I wonder when I shall be married, for
my beauty's beginning to fade.

Over the River Charlie

This lively game, harking back to the days of Bonny Prince Charlie, is another favorite of the play-parties, along with "Goin to Boston." One of these games usually called for the other, and Mom Ritchie remembers that, always after an evening of play-partying, where the only music was the singing of the players themselves (string music was sinful)--she was afflicted with a hoarse and very sore throat. The shuffling feet wore away the pine floor boards and filled the air in the room with dust, but they sang and played away and didn't even notice it, until the next day when, Mom tells me, they could always sweep up "a quart or two of dust and shavins." Floors had to be replaced often.

© 1940 by Geordie Music Publishing, Inc.

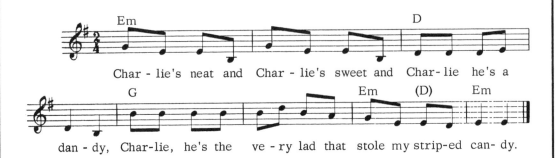

Char - lie's neat and Char - lie's sweet and Char - lie he's a

dan - dy, Char-lie, he's the ve - ry lad that stole my strip-ed can- dy.

CHORUS:

Over the river to feed my sheep,
Over the river, Charlie,
Over the river to feed my sheep
And to measure up my barley.

My pretty little pink, I once did think
I never could do without you;
Since I lost all hopes of you
I care very little about you.

(Chorus)

Don't want your wheat, don't want your
   cheat
And neither do I want your barley;
But I'll take a little of the best you've
   got
To bake a cake for Charlie.

(Chorus)

Barbry Ellen

This Ritchie version of "the song everybody knows" is our family adaptation of the tune and text that is found in the part of Knott County, Kentucky wherein my father, Balis Ritchie, was born and raised, and where the first twelve of us were born. We knew at least three other tunes in the family, but this one is my own favorite.

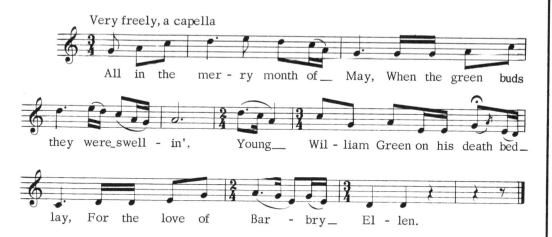

He sent his servant to the town
To the place where she was dwellin'
Sayin', Master's sick and he sends
  for you
If your name be Barbry Ellen.

So slow-lie, slow-lie she got up
And slow-lie she came a-nigh him
And all she said when she got there
Young man, I believe you're dyin'.

Oh yes, I'm low, I'm very low,
And death is on me dwellin',
No better, no better I'll never be
If I can't get Barbry Ellen.

Oh yes, you're low and very low,
And death is on you dwellin'
No better, no better you'll never
  be
For you can't get Barbry Ellen.

For don't you remember in yonder's
  town
In yonder's town a-drinkin',
You passed your glass all around
  and around
And you slighted Barbry Ellen.

Oh yes I remember in yonder's town
In yonder's town a-drinkin'
I gave my health to the ladies all
  around
But my heart to Barbry Ellen.

He turned his pale face to the wall
For death was on him dwellin'
Adieu, adieu, you good neighbors all
Adieu, sweet Barbry Ellen.

As she as goin' across the fields
She heard those death bells a-kneelin'
And every stroke the death bell give
Hard hearted Barbry Ellen.

Oh mother, oh mother, go make my
  bed,
Go make it both long and narrow
Young William's died for me today
And I'll die for him tomorrow.

Oh she was buried 'neath the old church
  tower
And he was buried a-nigh her
And out of his bosom grew a red, red
  rose,
Out of Barbry's grew a green briar.

They grew and they grew up the old
  church tower,
Until they could grow no higher
They locked and tied in a true lover's
  knot,
Red rose wrapped around the green
  briar.

Lonesome Sea

My mother does not sing many ballads. She prefers church songs and play-party game songs, and has some favorite love laments. This ballad is really the only one she ever sang, to amount to anything, and I have a very strong memory of her going about the house, sweeping or straining the milk or rock-ing some baby, her voice taking the risings and fallings of this tune with unhurried and unthinking beauty, especially on lines of the refrain, "as she sailed upon the low and the lonesome low, as she sailed upon the lonesome sea."

There was a little ship and she sailed up-on the sea,___ And she went by the name of the Mer-ry Gold-en Tree, As she sailed up-on the low___ and the lone-some_ low,_ As she sailed up-on the lone-some___ sea.

There was another ship and she sailed
  upon the sea,
And she went by the name of The
  Turkish Robbery,
As she sailed upon the low and the
  lonesome low,
As she sailed upon the lonesome sea.

There was a little cabin boy upon The
  Golden Tree,
Said, Captain, oh Captain, what will
  you give to me,
If I sink them in the low and the
  lonesome low,
If I sink them in the lonesome sea.

Oh a half of my ship shall be made
  unto thee,
And my youngest daughter shall be
  wed unto thee,
If you sink them in the low and the
  lonesome low,
If you sink them in the lonesome sea.

He bowed upon his breast and away
  swum he,
Till he come to the ship called
  The Turkish Robbery,
Gonna sink you in the low and the
  lonesome low,
Gonna sink you in the lonesome sea.

Then out of his pocket an instrument
  he drew
And he bored nine holes for to let
  that water through,
For to sink them in the low and the
  lonesome low,
For to sink them in the lonesome sea.

Oh some had hats and some had caps,
And they tried for to stop these
  ferverish water gaps,
But he sunk them in the low and the
  lonesome low,
But he sunk them in the lonesome sea.

He bowed upon his breast and back
  swum he,
Till he come to the ship called
  The Merry Golden Tree,
As she sailed upon the low and the
  lonesome low,
As she sailed on the lonesome sea.

Oh captain, oh captain, pray draw me
  up on board,
Oh captain, oh captain, pray give me
  my reward,
For I've sunk them in the low and the
  lonesome low
For I've sunk them in the lonesome sea.

I'll never draw you up on board,
No I've never known a cabinboy to
  gain such reward,
Though you sunk them in the low and
  the lonesome low,
Though you sunk them in the lonesome
  sea.

If it weren't for the love of your
  daughter and your men,
I would do unto you what I've done
  unto them,
I would sink you in the low and the
  lonesome low,
I would sink you in the lonesome sea.

He bowed upon his breast and down
  sunk he,
Farewell, farewell to The Merry Golden
  Tree,
For I'm sinking in the low and the
  lonesome low,
For I'm sinking in the lonesome sea.

Cedar Swamp

About two or three times during the school year, the little two-room grade school which I attended in Viper would run a pie supper, to raise money for something the county didn't furnish (almost everything). I remember that the most agonizing time was the hour after we girls had placed our brightly-wrapped and beribboned pies on the auctioneer's table (the two teachers' desks pushed together), each had been given the number of her own pie with instructions to keep it a secret from the boys, and had been told to "wait in the schoolyard until the bell rings." The moonlight was a witchery; the shadows were alive with the happy shrieks of young children not quite able to bear the heady freedom of the soft wild night; and the only thing that kept the whole lot of us from bursting with sheer excitement and joy was our joining together in games, usually singing games so that we could shout to the top of our lungs, jump and skip, dance pretty in hopes he would notice us, and somehow manage, just barely, to wait for that bell.

Lively
D

Way low down in the ce-dar swamp, Wa-ters deep and
mud-dy, There I met a pret-ty lit-tle miss,
A7 D Chorus
There I kissed my hon-ey. Swing a la-dy up and down,
Swing a la-dy home,_ Swing a la-dy up and down, Swing a la-dy home.

Built my love a big fine house,
Built it in the garden;
Put her in and she jumped out,
Fare you well, my darlin'.

Black-eyed girl is mad at me,
Blue-eyed girl won't have me;
If I can't get the one I love
Guess I'll never marry.

The older she gets, the prettier she gets,
I tell you she's a honey;
Makes me work all through the week,
And get stove-wood on Sunday!

Hiram Hubbard

Hiram Hubbard (we pronounce it H'arm) is a true tale about a local happening. The killing took place a few miles from home and the song travelled abroad and was popular for many years. To this day, some believe that "H'arm Hubbard was not guilty," though others say that he was. It might be that he was. Songs have a way of taking up for bad men. I learned the song from Dad Ritchie, who told me that he gathered it up from three or four people who remembered bits of it, and then he put it back together. Within my lifetime, I have not heard anyone else sing it but him, Balis Ritchie.

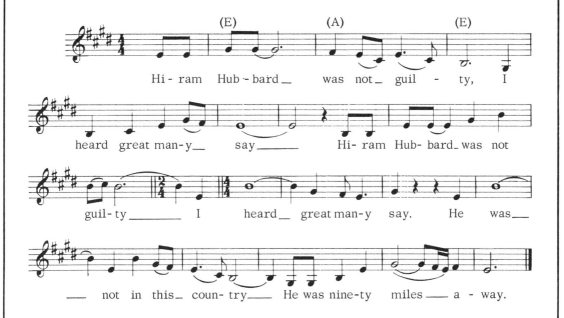

Hi-ram Hub-bard — was not — guil-ty, I heard great man-y — say — Hi-ram Hub-bard — was not guil-ty — I heard — great man-y say. He was — — not in this — coun-try — He was nine-ty miles — a - way.

While travelling through this country
  In sorrow and distress,
While travelling through this country
  In sorrow and distress,
The rebels overhauled him,
In chains they bound him fast.

They led him up the holler,
  They led him up the hill;
They led him up the holler,
  They led him up the hill
To the place of execution;
He begged to write his will.

They wound the cords around him,
  They bound him to the tree;
They wound the cords around him,
  They bound him to the tree;
Eleven balls went through him,
His body shrunk away.

Hiram Hubbard was not guilty
  I've heard great many say;
Hiram Hubbard was not guilty
  I've heard great many say;
He was not in this country,
He was ninety miles away.

Fair Annie of the Lochroyan

I have been told that this is a very rare ballad for this country, and that some of our words have never before been found in American versions, and only rarely in older British forms of the song. I can only say that it is a long song, and Uncle Jason told me that as such it was rarely sung all the way through except at play-parties during rest-times, when the ones who had a reputation for knowing the big ballads, would be called upon. The young man Jason would sing it then, and the boys would take that opportunity to "set in close to their girls, and all would listen with enjoyment to the story."

A capella

Oh — who will shoe my bon - ny— feet, And who will glove — my hand, ___ And who will kiss my ro - sy— cheeks, While you're in a far off land? Your Paw will shoe your— bon - ny feet, Your Maw will glove your— hand, And— I will kiss your ro - sy—. cheeks, When I ___ come back a - gain.

Oh who will build a bonny ship
And set her on the sea
For I will go and seek my love
My own love Gregory.
 Oh up and spoke her father dear
 And a wealthy man was he
 And he has built a bonny ship
 And set her on the sea.

Oh he has built a bonny ship
To sail upon the sea
The mast was of the beaten gold
As fine as it could be.
 She had not sailed but twenty
  leagues,
 But twenty leagues and three
 When she met with a rank robber
 And all of his company.

Are you the Queen of Heaven, he cried,
Come to pardon all our sins
Or are you the Merry Magdelene
That was born at Bethlehem?
 I'm not the Queen of Heaven, said she,
 Come to pardon all your sins
 Nor I'm the Merry Magdelene
 That was born at Bethlehem.

But I am the Lass of Lochroyan
That's sailing on the sea
To see if I can find my love
My own love Gregory.
 Oh see you now yon bonny bower
 All covered o'er with thyme
 And when you've sailed it around
  and about
 Lord Gregory is within.

Now row the boat my mariners
And bring me to the land
For it's now I see my true love's
    castle
Close by the salt sea strand.
    She sailed it 'round and sailed it
        'round
    And loud and long cried she
    Now break, now break your
        fairy charms
    And set my true love free.

She has taken her young son in her
    arms
And to the door she's gone
And long she's knocked and loud
    she's called
But answer she's got none.
    Open the door Lord Gregory
    Open and let me in
    The wind blows cold, blows cold,
        my love
    The rain drops from my chin.

The shoe is frozen to my feet
The glove unto my hand
The wet drops from my frozen hair
And I can scarce-lie stand.
    Up then and spoke his ill
        mother,
    As mean as she could be
    You're not the Lass of the
        Lochroyan
    She is far out o'er the sea.

Away, away, you ill woman,
You don't come here for good,
You're but some witch who strolls
    about
Or a mermaid of the flood.
    Now open the doors love Gregory
    Open the doors I pray
    For thy young son is in my arms
    And will be dead ere it is day.

Ye lie, ye lie, ye ill woman,
So loud I hear ye lie,
For Annie of the Lochroyan
Is far out o'er the sea
    Fair Annie turned her round and
        about
    Well since this all is so
    May never a woman that's bourne
        a son
    Have a heart so full of woe.

When the cock had crow'n and the day
    had dawned
And the sun begun to peep
Up then and raised Lord Gregory
And sore, sore die he weep.
    Oh I have dream't a dream
        mother
    The thought it grieves me great
    That Fair Annie of the Lochroyan
    Lay dead at my bed feet.

If it be for Annie of Lochroyan
You make all of this moan
She stood last night at your bower
    window
But I have sent her home
    Oh he's gone down unto the shore
    To see what he could see
    And there he saw fair Annie's
        barque
    Come a-roarin' o'er the sea.

Oh Annie, oh Annie, loud he cried
Oh Annie, oh Annie, my dear
But all the loud that he did cry
Fair Annie she could not hear.
    The wind blew loud, the waves rose
        high
    And dashed the boat on shore
    Fair Annie's corpse was in the foam
    The babe rose never more.

Then first he kissed her pale, pale
    cheeks
And then he kissed her chin
And then he kissed her cold, cold lips
There was no breath within.
    Oh woe betide my ill mother,
    An ill death may she die
    She has not been the death of one
    But she has been the death of three.

(Sung to second half of tune)

Then he took out a little dart
That hung down by his side
And thrust it through and through
    his heart
And then fell down and died.

The Gypsy Laddie

Most people know this as "The Wraggle-Taggle Gypsies," and as such it is very popular throughout the English-speaking world. This version I give you here will never have such wide acceptance, but it grows on one if given a chance. The tune is yours to sing as you like, free-style (as I sing it, with unannounced holds when I feel they are right for the words), or as brisk as you like, with steady beat. Like everything else I sing, I hardly if ever get through it the same way twice, which makes it a problem to write out the music of if. Anyway, here is the basic tune.

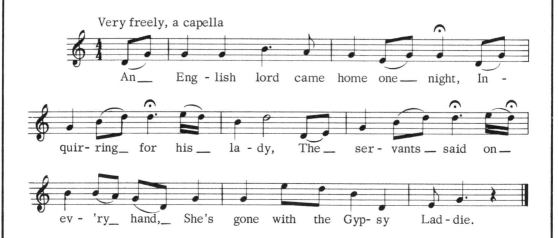

Very freely, a capella

An__ Eng-lish lord came home one__ night, In-quir-ring__ for his__ la-dy, The__ ser-vants__ said on__ ev-'ry__ hand,__ She's gone with the Gyp-sy Lad-die.

Go saddle up my milk-white steed,
Go saddle me up my brownie
And I will ride both night and day
Till I overtake my bonnie.

Oh he rode East and he rode West,
And at last he found her,
She was lying on the green, green grass
And the Gypsy's arms all around her.

Oh, how can you leave your house
   and land,
How can you leave your money,
How can you leave your rich young
   lord
To be a gypsy's bonnie.

How can you leave your house and
   land,
How can you leave your baby,
How can you leave your rich young
   lord
To be a gypsy's lady.

Oh come go home with me, my dear,
Come home and be my lover,
I'll furnish you with a room so neat,
With a silken bed and covers.

I won't go home with you, kind sir,
Nor will I be your lover,
I care not for your rooms so neat
Or your silken bed or your covers.

It's I can leave my house and land,
And I can leave my baby,
I'm a-goin' to roam this world around
And be a gypsy's lady.

Oh, soon this lady changed her mind,
Her clothes grew old and faded,
Her hose and shoes came off her feet
And left them bare and naked.

Just what befell this lady now,
I think it worth relating,
Her gypsy found another lass
And left her heart a-breaking.

Old King Cole

Dad Ritchie called this one "a gettin-up game." He and Mom and the other courting couples would use it to start the evening's party off when everyone was too bashful to take partners. At last, one brave couple would promenade round the room singing this song, and when they got to the line, "We'll open up the ring and choose a couple in," another boy would have got up nerve to ask a girl up, and they'd come in. Then the four of them would begin the game-song all over again, and keep it up until they had enough players on the floor for "Boston" or "Charlie."

© 1953 by BMI

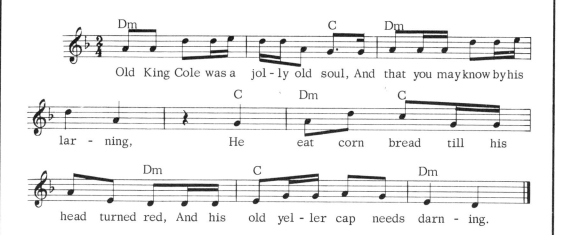

Old King Cole was a jol-ly old soul, And that you may know by his lar-ning, He eat corn bread till his head turned red, And his old yel-ler cap needs darn-ing.

My pretty little pink, I once did think
That I and you would marry,
But now I've lost all hopes of you
And I ain't got long to tarry.

I'll take my knapsack on my back,
My musket on my shoulder;
I'll march away to Mexico,
Enlist and be a soldier.

Where the coffee grows on the white
  oak tree
And the rivers they run brandy;
Where the boys are pure as a lump
  of gold
And the girls are sweet as candy.

You may go on and I'll turn back
To the place where we first parted;
We'll open up the ring and choose a
  couple in
And we hope they'll come free-hearted.

Somebody

Mom Ritchie once told me how she learned "Somebody" originally. She was sixteen, and engaged to be married. "It was a hard matter to keep my mind of book learning...I'd set with my eyes on the snowy hills and dream about my wedding day...what it would be like...about how long off and how close up it seemed, and I'd wonder what kind of cloth Pap would bring for my dress...bout the only thing I did learn that winter was...one day some of us girls were walking together at recess and Mary Cornett, she got to singing at a little song. Foolish little thing, but I got struck on the words and that evening I walked home with her and made her sing it over until I learnt it. After that I sung it around the house so much that Mammy Sally threatened to whup me if I didn't hush." Mom changed the song to suit her own situation and to describe the young Balis Ritchie more truly.

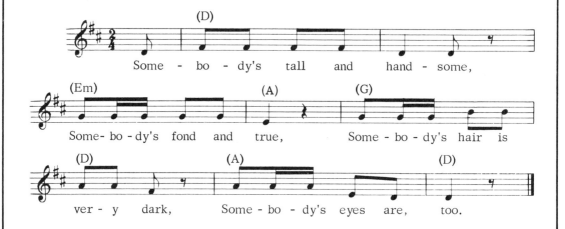

Some - bo - dy's tall and hand - some,
Some - bo - dy's fond and true,
Some - bo - dy's hair is ver - y dark,
Some - bo - dy's eyes are, too.

I love somebody fondly,
I love somebody true;
I love somebody with all my heart,
He loves somebody, too.

Somebody called to see me,
Somebody called last night;
Somebody asked me to be his bride,
And of course I said, All right.

I am somebody's darling,
I am somebody's pride,
And the day is not far-distant
When I'll be somebody's bride.

Somebody's tall and handsome,
Somebody's fond and true;
Somebody's hair is very dark,
Somebody's eyes are, too.

Dance to Your Daddy

I never thought much of this little tune, one way or another. I can remember Dad holding my hands and "dancing" me around the kitchen floor as he sang it, when I was very little. He would give all the little ones a turn at it--my nephews and nieces were always visiting, for they lived nearby, and, my sister Ollie having been married before I was born, a few of these nephews and nieces were a little older than I!--and I remember that we would laugh and tease each other because, whether he was "dancing" a boy or a girl, he always sang it, "laddie," and "little man." The second verse was added years later by my own little man, Peter Pickow, when he was two and a half. He said he felt that Mommy should also be danced to, so he and I made up a "Dance to your Mammy" verse.

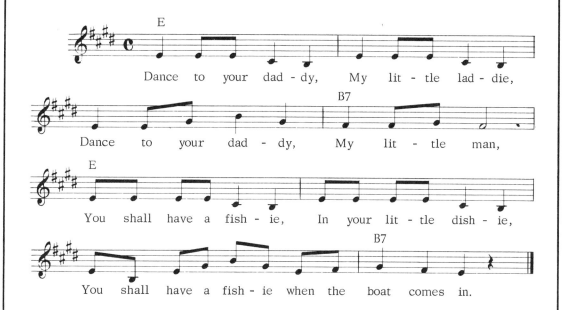

Dance to your dad - dy, My lit - tle lad - die,
Dance to your dad - dy, My lit - tle man,
You shall have a fish - ie, In your lit - tle dish - ie,
You shall have a fish - ie when the boat comes in.

Dance to your mammy,
My little lambie,
Dance to your mammy
My bonny lamb;
You shall have a suppie
In your little cuppie,
You shall have a suppie
When the cow comes home.

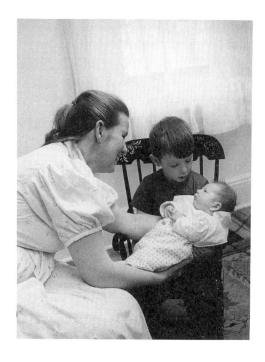

My Little Carpenter

This old ballad has been sung in our family for generations. My mother sang a different version, a sweeter tune. This one is mine, descended from my sister Una's and Uncle Jason's. Their two tunes were similar, and I soon got them well commingled in my mind. The result is a glorious hard–driving banjo tune and a grand tragic story.

Well met, well met, my own true love, Well met, well met, said he, I've come from far a-cross the sea, And it's all for the sake of thee.

I could have married a King's daughter fair,
And she would've married me,
But I have forsaken the crowns of gold
And it's all for the sake of thee.

If you could've married a king's daughter fair,
I'm sure I'm not to blame,
For I have married me a little carpenter
And I'm sure he's a fine young man.

Oh will you leave your little carpenter
And sail away with me
I'll take you to where the grass grows green
Down in sweet Italy.

Oh if I leave my little carpenter,
And sail away with ye,
What will ye have to maintain me upon
When we are far away.

Oh I have seven ships upon the sea
Seven ships upon the land
Four hundred and fifty bold sailor men
To be at your command.

She turned herself three times around
She kissed her babies three,
Farewell, farewell you sweet little babes
Keep your father sweet company.

They hadn't been sailin' but about two weeks,
I'm sure it was not three
When this fair lady begin for to weep
And she wept most bitterly.

Are you weepin for your little carpenter
Are you weepin for your store
Or are you weepin' for your sweet little babes,
That you never shall see any more.

Not a-weepin' for my little carpenter
Not a-weepin' for my store
Yes, I'm weepin' for my sweet little babes
That I never will see any more.

They hadn't been sailin' but about three weeks,
I'm sure it was not four,
When the ship sprung a leak and down she sank
And she sank to rise no more.

What hills, what hills so fair and
  so bright,
What hills so white and fair?
Oh those be the hills of heaven,
  my dear,
But you won't never go there.

What hills, what hills down in yonder
  sea,
What hills so black as coal?
Oh those be the hills of hell, my dear,
Where we must surely go.

I wish I never had seen your face,
I wish I'd never seen your gold,
I wish I was back to my little carpenter,
For he never would use me so.

Bangum Rid by the Riverside

Aunt Ellen Fields, kinswoman on our Mother's side, first sang for me this fine lilting version of Old Bangum, or, as he is named in Child's ballad number 18, Sir Lionel. She said her father used to sing it to her and her brothers and sisters when they were children, as he'd trot them on his knee. She had only two or three fragmentary verses and the "cuddle down" chorus; I have, in singing it over the years, added enough to piece out the story, from Uncle Jason's and our own family's similarly sketchy versions.

©1965 by Geordie Music Publishing, Inc.

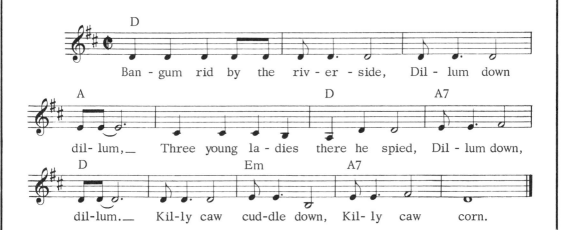

Ban- gum rid by the riv- er- side, Dil- lum down
dil- lum,__ Three young la - dies there he spied, Dil - lum down,
dil-lum.__ Kil- ly caw cud-dle down, Kil- ly caw corn.

There's a wild boar in these woods,
Who'll eat his meat, 'll suck his blood.

If you would this wild boar see
Blow a blast, he'll come to thee.

Slapped the horn into his mouth,
Blew a blast both North and South.

Wild boar come in such a rush,
Split his way through oak and ash.

Fit four hours by the day,
At last the wild boar run away.

Old Bangum follered him to his den,
Saw the bones of a thousand men.

Cambridgeshire May Song

In Stratford-Upon-Avon, England, in 1953, Mr. Russell Wortley sang for me this lovely carol. It has been sung for centuries by young men and girls in Cambridgeshire on May Day mornings. The "may," green boughs and spring flowers, is gathered the night before, or very early on May Day Morning, and carried by the group from house to house throughout the village. At each cottage the song is sung, the may is hung over the door to insure prosperity, health and food farm yields for the coming year. Then the carolers pass their money-box and walk along to the next house.

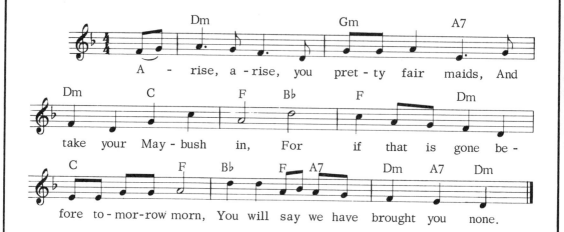

A - rise, a - rise, you pret - ty fair maids, And take your May - bush in, For if that is gone be - fore to - mor - row morn, You will say we have brought you none.

O the hedges and the fields are growing
  so green,
As green as grass can be;
Your Heavenly Father He watereth them
With His Heavenly dews so sweet.

I have a little purse in my pocket;
It's tied with a silver string.
And all that I lack is a little of your
  silver
To line it well within.

O the clock is striking one, it's time
  we were gone,
We can no longer stay;
So please to remember our money,
  money box,
And increase it whilst you may.

Mama Told Me

There are three or four songs in our locality about the disadvantages of a young girl's marrying an old man. The others are more or less laments, cursing the mother for insisting on the match, and so on. "An Old Man Came Courtin Me," is the only other one besides this that is downright funny. My sister Una used to sing, "Mama Told Me" to us young'uns, and it was and is still thought of in our family as a children's song.

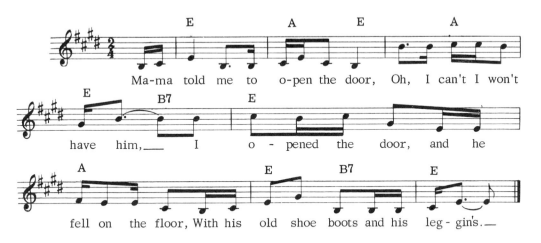

Ma-ma told me to o-pen the door, Oh, I can't I won't have him, ___ I o - pened the door, and he fell on the floor, With his old shoe boots and his leg - gins. ___

Mama told me to bring him a chair,
  O, I can't I won't have him!
I brought him a chair and Lord! how he
  did stare.
  With his old shoe-boots and his
  leggins.

Mama told me to bring him a plate,
  O, I can't I won't have him!
I brought him a plate and he kicked it
  in the grate
  With his old shoe-boots and his
  leggins.

Mama told me to bring him a fork,
  I brought him a fork and he asked
  me to go to New York.

Mama told me to bring him a knife,
  I brought him a knife and he asked
  me to be his wife.

Mama told me to fix him some meat;
  I fixed him some meat and Lord!
  how he did eat.

Mama told me to make up his bed,
  I made up his bed and I wisht that
  he was dead.

Mama told me to cover him well,
  I covered him well and he snored like
  the devil.

Black Is The Color

My older sisters learned this song while attending the John C. Campbell Folk School in Brasstown, North Carolina, and they brought it back to Kentucky and the family. We have loved it ever since. It was collected in 1916 by Cecil Sharp, from Mrs. Lizzie Roberts at Hot Springs, North Carolina, and appears in Sharp's splendid collection, English Folk-Songs of the Southern Appalachians.

Traditional

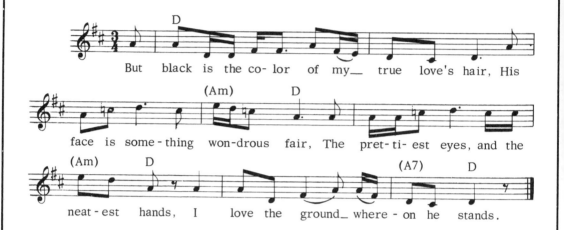

But black is the co-lor of my__ true love's hair, His face is some-thing won-drous fair, The pret-ti-est eyes, and the neat-est hands, I love the ground__ where-on he stands.

I love my love and well he knows,
I love the ground whereon he goes,
If you on earth no more I see
I can't serve you as you have me.

The winter's past and the leaves are
    green,
The time is past that we have seen,
But still I hope the time will come
When you and I shall be as one.

My own true love, so fare you well,
The time has come, but I wish you well,
But still I hope the time would come
When you and I shall be as one.

I go to the Clyde for to mourn, to weep,
But satisfied I never can sleep;
I'll write to you in a few little lines,
I'll suffer death ten thousand times.

But black is the color of my truelove's
    hair,
His face is something wondrous fair,
The prettiest eyes and the neatest
    hands.
I love the ground whereon he stands.

Lovin' Henry

As a child I used to go cow-hunting up to the head of our holler. Many times, after starting the cows on towards home, I'd take the side road down to Aunt Mary Ann's house, drawn by the sounds of singing and the good smell of browning cornbread as my cousins cooked supper. Maybe I'd get there in time to help them finish whatever they were singing, and one I loved was the ballad about Lovin' Henry (a song the family had brought back from their covered-wagon trip to Arkansas). And maybe I'd get a hot buttered hoe-cake to eat on the way home! © 1971 Adapted and arranged by Jean Ritchie/Ritchie Family

Light down, light down—— lov - ing Hen - ry she cried, And

stay all—— night with me. The gold - en—— cords a -

round my—— bed will—— be sup - plied to thee.

Light down, light down, lovin' Henry
  she cried
And stay all night with me;
The golden cords all around my bed
Shall be supplied to thee.

I can't light down, I can't light down
And stay all night with thee,
For I have a little girl in the old Scotland
And tonight she's a-lookin for me.

Lean down, lean down, lovin' Henry
  she cried
And give a sweet kiss to me,
And then you may ride to the old Scotland
And ride the more merrily.

Well he leant down and they kissed
  so sweet,
She had her knife so sharp;
She wound her arms all around and
  around
And stabbed him to the heart.

Ride on, ride on, lovin' Henry she said
Beneath the moon and the sun,
And your little girl can weep for you
And I hope she will weep alone.

I can't ride on, Lady Margret he said,
Beneath the moon nor the sun.
If there are physicians in your land
I pray you to bring me a-one.

There's no physicians in all of this land
Can cure such a deadly wound;
But if I had a hundred at my command
I would not bring you a-one.

She's call-ed to her waiting men
And to her waiting maids,
There's lying a dead man down in the road–
I pray you to take him away.

Some took him by his long yellow hair,
Some took him by his feet,
They sunk him down to the bottom of the well
It was so dark and deep.

Lay there, lay there, you falsehearted man,
Till the flesh rots off your bones,
And that little girl in the old Scotland
Will think long of your coming home.

There sits a little bird in the willow tree
She sings so clear and shrill,
That fair young man from the old Scotland
Lies dead in my lady's well.

Fly down, fly down, you pretty little bird
And sit upon my knee,
Your cage shall be of the finest yellow gold
With bands of ivory.

I won't fly down, no I won't fly down
And sit upon your knee,
For as you have killed your own truelove
I fear that you would kill me.

O I wish I had my bended bow
With an arrow in the string,
I'd shoot it through your tender little heart
So none could hear you sing.

Well it's if you had your bended bow
With an arrow in the string,
I'd rise up high, high above your mark
And there my song I'd sing.

The Reckless and Rambling Boy

This is a banjo-picking song and therefore considered unladylike by my mother. We girls usually heard it sung on still Sunday afternoons as we walked up and down the roads listening to the young boys of the community at their Sunday get-togethers—usually a banjo and fiddle-playing session on some deserted store porch. Both Dad and Uncle Jason remember it from their boy-hood, and Justus Begley sang it. I have gathered all their versions together here, and in doing so am struck with the similarity of some of the lyrics with the song, "But Black Is The Color of My Truelove's Hair." I have published this song before, in a shortened version. Here are all the verses I have found. © 1971 Jean Ritchie/ Geordie Music Pub. Co.

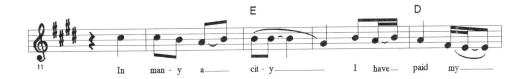

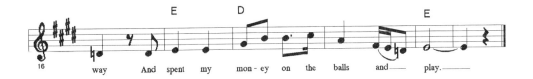

It's I am a reckless and rambling boy,
Through many a time and a show I have
  been;
In many a city I have paid my way
And spent my money on the balls and play.

In Cumberland City I married me a wife,
I loved her as I loved my life.
She treated me kindly by night and by day
And she caused me to rob on the King's
  Highway.

O that pretty little girl, sixteen years old,
Hair just as yeller as the flaming gold.
Well the prettiest face and sweetest hands,
God bless the ground onwhere she stands.

I robbed them all I will declare,
I robbed them all in deep despair;
I robbed them all ten thousand pound
One night when I was rambling around.

O I love you well, and so well you know,
I love the ground onwhere you go;
If pleasures no more on this earth I see
I wouldn't serve you as you're a-serving me.

So my pretty little girl, so fare you well,
You say we are quit but I wish you well,
For I live in hopes that the time will come
When you and I can live as one.

O it's down by the river I'll mourn and weep
For I'm satisfied that I can not sleep,
But I'll write to you just a few short lines,
It's worse than death ten thousand times.

I'll buy me some paper and I'll sit down,
And I'll write up a letter to the Governor's
    town;
He'll receive that letter and he'll read it
    awhile
And begin to think on his woman and child.

Then I'll buy me a ticket in this old foreign
    town,
Get me a seat and it's I'll sit down,
Well the wheels will roll and the whistles
    will blow,
Take me a long time to get back home.

Well I've got the money for to carry me
    through,
A fine broad sword and a pistol too,
A forty-five that never fails,
And a black-eyed girl from the land of Wales.

My father he sits and weeps and mourns,
My mother declares she is left alone,
And that false-hearted girl with the curly
    hair,
She wrings her hands all in despair.

I'll get another paper and I'll sit down,
Write me a letter up to London town.
Let the people read, let the people cry,
Here's an innocent boy too young to die.

Come old and young and stand around
And see me laid in this cold ground.
I'm not ashamed nor afraid to die
But I hope to meet you by and by.

Her Mantle So Green

Uncle Jason had two verses of this Irish song, remembered from his grandparents: the first verse, and the one beginning, "He turned back her mantle. . . ." Over the years, I have come to know the story, and that it is yet another "broken token" ballad, in which the returning soldier or sailor disguises himself until he has proved to himself that his love has been true all these years. This one is delightfully different in that, instead of a ring or half a handkerchief, the proof is her embroidery, his name "emblazed on her mantle so green." I have collected some lines, and written others, to finish out the story. © 1996 Jean Ritchie/Geordie Music Pub. Co.

As I went out walk-ing so ear-ly in— Spring,

To see the new flow-ers— and to hear the birds sing——

I spied a fair dam-sel,— she ap-peared like a— queen

In cost-ly fine rai-ment and her man-tle so— green.

As I went out walking so early in spring
To see the new flowers and to hear the
    birds sing,
I spied a fair damsel, she appeared like a
    queen
In her costly fine raiment and her mantle
    so green.

I said, O fair creature, you have my heart
    beguiled,
And I'm bound for to ask you to become my
    dear wife.
She anwered me, Kind sir, I must you
    refuse,
For my truelove fell a-fighting in famed
    Waterloo.

O who was your truelove, come tell me his name,
For it is from that battle so lately I came.
Sir, turn back my mantle and there will be seen
His name all embroidered on my mantle so green.

He turned back her mantle and there did behold
His own name and his surname in letters of gold,
His own name and his surname so plain to be seen
Emblazed on her mantle, on her mantle so green.

Rise up, dearest Molly, your fears I'll remove
Since true you've been to me, and tis you that I love.
Now the wars are all over, no more to be seen,
And I'll wed my fair lady in her mantle so green—
And you'll shine like a jewel in your mantle so green. (Repeat melody of preceding line)

Loving Hannah

Older menfolk in the Ritchie family, rather than the women for some unknown reason, sang this song: Balis, my Dad, and his cousins Jason and Isom Ritchie. In the sixties, banjo players were singing a more modern version, "Handsome Molly." People ask us about "a bally boat," named in our last verse. Some guess it means *bar-* *ley* boat, but my guess is that "bally" is a Celtic word meaning handsome or pretty—in other words, "a fine, pretty boat." At any rate, "Loving Hannah" is a fine, pretty song, and one of my enduring favorites. © 1965 Jean Ritchie/Geordie Music Pub. Co.

I rode to church last Sunday, my truelove
  passed me by,
I knew her mind was a-changing by the
  roving of her eye.
    By the roving of her eye, by the roving of
    her eye,
    I knew her mind was a-changing by the
    roving of her eye.

My love is fair and proper, her hands and
  feet are small
And she is quite good-looking, and that's
  the best of all
    And that's the best of all, and that's the
    best of all,
    And she is quite good-looking, and that's
    the best of all.

O Hannah, loving Hannah, come give to
    me your hand,
You said if you ever married, that I would
    be the man.
    That I would be the man, that I would be
      the man,
    You said if you ever married, that I
      would be the man.

I'll go down by the waters when everyone
    is asleep,
I'll think of loving Hannah, and then sit
    down and weep.
    And then sit down and weep, and then
      sit down and weep,
    I'll think of loving Hannah, and then sit
      down and weep.

I wish I were in London or some other
    seaport town,
I'd set my foot on a bally boat and I'd sail
    them seas all around
    I'd sail them seas all around, I'd sail
      them seas all around,
    I'd set my foot on a bally boat and I'd sail
      them seas all around.

Audiography

This is a selected audiography representing only the recordings that are currently available. Other recordings may be obtained through selected libraries.

British Traditional Ballads (Child Ballads) in the Southern Mountains (1960); Smithsonian/Folkways 02301, 02302

Childhood Songs (1991); Greenhays GR90723 (available only on cassette)

High Hills and Mountains (1979); Greenhays GR70708 (available on compact disc with *None but One*)

Jean Ritchie and Doc Watson at Folk City (1963); Smithsonian/Folkways CDSF 4005

Jean Ritchie Sings Childrens Songs and Games from the Southern Mountains (1957); Smithsonian/Folkways 07054

Kentucky Christmas Old and New (1990); Greenhays GR70717 (cassette and compact disc)

The Most Dulcimer (1984); Greenhays GR CD70714

Mountain Born (1995); Greenhays Recordings GR70725 (cassette and compact disc)

None but One (1977); Greenhays GR70708 (available on a compact disc with *High Hills and Mountains*)

Precious Memories (1962); Smithsonian/Folkways 02427

The Ritchie Family of Kentucky (1959); Smithsonian/Folkways 02316

Sweet Rivers (1981); June Appal JA0037C (available only on cassette)

To order:

June Appal
306 Madison Street
Whitesburg, KY 41858

Telephone: (606) 633-0108

Greenhays Recordings (distributed by Rounder Recordings)
7A Locust Avenue
Port Washington, NY 11050

Smithsonian/Folkways
414 Hungerford Drive
Suite 444
Rockville, MD 20850

Telephone (800) 410-9815
Web site: HTTP://www.si.edu/folkways

Videography

Backgrounds (1986); Produced by Folklife Productions; George Pickow, producer. Available from Greenhays Recordings.

Mountain Born (1996); Produced by KET, The Kentucky Network; H. Russell Farmer and Guy Mendes, producers.

To order from KET:

Kentucky Educational Television
600 Cooper Drive
Lexington, KY 40502-2296

Telephone: (606) 258-7000

Note: With KET's permission, Greenhays is also offering the *Mountain Born* video with an additional forty minutes of *Jean Ritchie in Performance through the Years*. This version may be ordered through Greenhays Recordings.

Index to Recorded Songs

Abbreviations

The Gypsie Laddie	CB1
The Hangman Song	CB1
Her Mantle So Green	
Hiram Hubbard	RD
The Holly Bears the Berry	
I Saw Three Ships	KC
I've Got a Mother Gone To Glory	SR
I Wonder When I Shall Be Married	RF
Joe Bowers	RF
Jubilee	MD
Keep Your Garden Clean	
Killy Kranky	MD
Little Bitty Baby (Children Go Where I Send Thee)	KC
Little Cory	
The Little Devils	CB2
The Little Musgrave	CB2
London Bridge	RF
Lonesome Sea	CB1, RF
Lord Lovel	CB1
Lord Randal	CB2
Lord Thomas and Fair Ellender	CB1, RF
Love Somebody, Yes I Do	SG, MB
Loving Hannah	MB
Lovin' Henry	
Mama Told Me	SG
The May Day Carol	
The Miracle of Usher's Well	CB2
My Little Carpenter	CB1, RD
Nottamun Town	NO
Oh, Love Is Teasin'	
Old Betty Larkin	
Old King Cole	SG
The Old Soap-Gourd	SG
Old Virginny	
The Old Woman and the Pig	
Over the River, Charlie	MD
Pretty Saro	MD, RF
The Reckless and Rambling Boy	
See the Waters A-Gliding	
Shady Grove	CS
Sister Phoebe	
Skin and Bones	CS
Somebody	RF
The Swapping Song	CS, SG
Sweet William and Lady Margaret	CB2
There Was a Pig Went Out To Dig	
The Turkish Lady	CB1, RF
Twilight A-Stealing	RF
Two Dukes A-Roving	SG
The Unquiet Grave	CB2
What'll I Do with This Baby-O?	RD